THE
STORY OF INDIAN MUSIC
AND ITS
INSTRUMENTS

Plate I.

A POPULAR DECCAN ORCHESTRA. The tambourine player is seated performing at an Indian fête held in the author's compound. at the extreme left of the group.

Frontispiece.

THE
STORY OF INDIA MUSIC

AND ITS
INSTRUMENTS

A Study of the Present &
A Record of the Past

TOGETHER WITH SIR WILLIAM JONES' CELEBRATED
TREATISE IN FULL, WITH 19 PLATES CHIEFLY OF
INSTRUMENTS, MUSIC ILLUSTRATIONS AND A MAP

By
Ethel Rosenthal

LOW PRICE PUBLICATIONS
Delhi-110052

Distributed by
D K Publishers Distributors P Ltd.
24, Ansari Road, Darya Ganj,
New Delhi-110002
Phones: 23261465, 23278584, 23201514
Fax : 23264368
visit us at: www.dkpd.com
e-mail: dkpd@del3.vsnl.net.in

First Published 1928

Reprinted in LPP 1993, 1996, 2003

ISBN 81-7536-308-8

Published by
Low Price Publications
A-6, Nimri Commercial Centre,
Near Ashok Vihar Phase-IV,
Delhi-110052
Phone: 27401672, 27452453
visit us at: www.lppindia.com
e-mail: lpp@nde.vsnl.net.in

Printed at
D K Fine Art Press P Ltd.
Delhi-110052

PRINTED IN INDIA

TO His Highness the Maharáj Rana Sir Bhawani
Singh of Jhalawar, K.C.S.I., F.Z.S., F.R.G.S.,
M.R.A.S., etc.

His Highness has honoured me by accepting the dedication of this work on Indian music.

His appreciation of art, literature and science is well known in India, and in each of the many countries in which he has travelled. An ardent supporter of Indian music, he has permitted his name to appear on the lists of donors of the Third and Fourth All-India Music Conferences, besides encouraging musicians from his State to participate in the Conference programmes.

Owing to the personal interest taken by His Highness in all forms of educational development, Jhalrapatan,* the capital of Jhalawar State, is a centre of literary activity.

ETHEL ROSENTHAL.

Secunderabad, Deccan.

MCMXXVIII.

---

* *Jhalrapatan*, means " City of Bells," and, according to Colonel Tod, the author of " Annals and Antiquities of Rajast'han," is so named because of the large number of temple bells heard in the old city.

FOREWORD

THE present work, an outline sketch of the subject, does not claim to be a comprehensive study of Indian music. The chapters were written primarily with a view to stimulating interest in Indian music, in the hope that English readers already acquainted with the subject might be encouraged to pursue their studies further, while new recruits might be added to the small group of Western music lovers, prepared to further the cause of Indian music. The author has not attempted to treat the subject exhaustively, but has endeavoured, rather, to enumerate some of the many attractive features which emphasise the charm, dignity and interest of Indian music.

The soul of a nation is revealed through the medium of its art, and appreciation of that art promotes sympathy for the land from which it springs. It is through the medium of Indian music that the author has striven to acquire some comprehension of the psychology of the Indian people and of the Land of Wonders—where she has spent several years of enthralling interest. Perchance, this book may act as a link to reinforce the chain which unites music-lovers of East and West. If so, the author will be amply repaid for her labour of love. She has tried to acknowledge all sources of information, and has compiled the bibliography for the assistance of readers anxious to consult those sources for themselves.

The warmest thanks of the author are due to many friends in India for their valuable assistance. Space does not permit of individual mention of each helper who ungrudgingly placed time and talent at her disposal. She is as much indebted to those who urged her to proceed with her studies, as to those who offered her material aid, by affording her opportunities to become acquainted personally with Indian musicians, and to attend their performances.

The several languages current in India, the decay of records due to climatic conditions, and the illiteracy of a vast percentage of the population create many hindrances to the research worker, anxious to obtain, from local sources, reliable information respecting Indian music. Owing to the many tongues spoken in various quarters of the Indian Empire,

and to diverse forms of orthography, the spelling
of Indian words presents grave difficulties to the
foreigner.   The author apologises for her ignorance,
and for having failed to conform to the Hunterian
system of transliterating vernacular names. She
craves the indulgence of Indian readers, should they
observe names in unfamiliar guise and unaccented.
The lack of standardised methods, which constitutes
a stumbling-block to the Indian engaged in the study
of Hindustani and Carnatic music, presents an ob-
stacle wellnigh insuperable to the European. Should
this work contain statements which are not in con-
formity with the views of some authorities on Indian
music, the author would recall the many contro-
versial problems relating to the art, on which even
learned pandits are at variance.

She is particularly grateful for the privilege accorded her of access to the magnificent Parmanand
Library at Jhalrapatan, where many valuable works
now out of print were consulted, and for the kind
permission granted for the view of the *naubat khána*
to be taken expressly to illustrate this work.

CONTENTS.

LIST OF ILLUSTRATIONS.

LIST OF ILLUSTRATIONS.

LIST OF ILLUSTRATIONS.

INTRODUCTION.[*]

THE Vindhya mountains form a natural barrier between Hindustan and the Deccan. The differences between the inhabitants of Northern and Southern India are considerable, and the two great divisions of Indian music, into the Hindustani, or Northern, school and the Carnatic, or Southern, school must not be overlooked by any foreigner, who would become acquainted with the classification of *rágas* or melody modes. All *rágas* express certain *rásas*, or emotions; when their language is understood, the soul of Indian music is revealed in all its beauty. Yet Indian music must be regarded as a whole—albeit a composite whole—if its full import is to be comprehended, for it reflects the varying

---

[*] To obviate the necessity for lengthy footnotes, the author has deemed it permissible to incorporate in the introduction certain information collected from local sources, since the original chapters were written.

characteristics of a people who have submitted to widely divergent influences. Owing to his geographical position, the northerner has been more directly affected by foreign elements than his Dravidian brother of the south, yet the same spirituality underlies the finest and best in music, both north and south, and this same spirituality constitutes a bond of sympathy between Asiatic and European musicians, who believe in the sanctity of their art. In Hindu lore, the invention of numerous musical instruments is attributed to the gods, and the affection of Indian musicians for their *vínás*, flutes and drums is similar to the devotion which Western instrumentalists bestow upon their pianos, violins and 'cellos. The affection of the European concert artist, however, is usually of a practical nature, and is evidenced by the trouble which he takes to maintain his instrument in perfect condition. The devotion of the Indian performer is possibly more idealistic. Perchance his love for his instrument blinds him to its defects, while he is hampered further by a lack of reliable makers to whom he could entrust his instrument for repair.

The modern tendency to combine the northern and southern systems is significant of the unity which constitutes the bedrock of Indian music as a whole. The systematisation of *rágas*, and the fusion of the northern and southern methods, are subjects which have figured on the agenda of the All-India Music Conferences. Attempts are being made also to introduce the study of music into the curricula of primary and secondary schools and colleges. All these measures augur well for a much-needed renaissance in Indian music, and if, or when, the proposal to found a musical academy in New Delhi materialises, it seems probable that the future welfare of Indian music will be assured.

Owing to absence of harmony and to unfamiliar melodic progressions, due to the employment of microtones, and the general absence of the tempered scale, it is no easy matter for a European to appreciate Indian music at a first hearing. As his ear becomes attuned to Eastern airs, however, the Westerner realises that freedom of melody compensates for lack of harmony, and learns to estimate the drone at its true value. The heart of Indian music is its melody, and, to become sensitised to its charm, the Western ear must accustom itself to the employment of grace notes as a means of characterisation. Grace in Indian music is essential, not accidental, and supplies the *chiaroscuro* which harmony furnishes in Western compositions.

There is reason to believe that Indian art, letters and science were at their zenith between the fourth and the eighth centuries A.D., and it is probable that the apex of Indian music was reached about the same period. In the world-famous cave temples of Ajanta, situated in the north-west of the dominions of His Exalted Highness the Nizam of Hyderabad, there are many carvings representing musicians and dancers. Cave I at Ajanta, dating probably from the commencement of tne seventh century, was designed as a Buddhist monastery, and amongst its wealth of sculptural decoration, figure musical instruments, such as drums, flutes and trumpets. Possibly one of the causes which has contributed to the fall of music from its high estate is the absence of standard notation. The vital question of notation has aroused much discussion at every conference on Indian music, held during the past decade. Despite the Indian's inherited facility for memorising, the treasures of Indian national music cannot be preserved satisfactorily until the problem of notation has been solved, although phonographs and gramophones serve a useful purpose.

In India, there is a vast profusion of folk music which varies according to locality. In the south, songs are employed on every occasion, and, before it is too late, steps should be taken for the systematic collection and preservation of melodies forming some of the most precious records extant of Indian pastoral life. Until_all important Sanskrit and Hindustani treatises on music have been translated into European languages, together with works in Tamil, Telugu and Canarese, it will be impossible for a thorough knowledge of the theory of Hindustani and Carnatic music to be diffused amongst Western musicians. Such a task, although of formidable proportions, would be worthy of the attention of wealthy patrons, desirous of spreading appreciation of Indian art and culture. In the past, Indian music flourished, owing to the assistance which rich and cultured noblemen accorded to the artists who entertained them. Thus, untrammelled by material cares, musicians were enabled to give of their best, and to live for their art, and it is to be hoped that Indian magnates will not only continue, but increase, their support and encouragement of high-class musical performers, for it would be a sad day for Indian music should the musical profession become as distressingly overcrowded in India as it is in Europe. If the demand for highly-trained artists increases, the work of the All-India Music Conferences for the uplift of Indian music will be greatly facilitated.

The following notes on the life of Govinda Márár, obtained recently from Pandharpur, through the courtesy of an Indian gentleman residing near this town, supplement the references to Govinda Márár on pages 48 and 49 of this work.

Govinda Márár, known also as Govind Baba Beri, died at Pandharpur, after his visit to Thiruvaiyar, to pay his respects to Tyágarája. Some of the oldest inhabitants of Pandharpur, who remember reports, heard in their youth, of Govinda Márár's wonderful singing, recount the following incident. While Govinda Márár was living at Pándharpur, the Maharája of Gwalior, accompanied by a Muhammadan vocalist who sang daily in the *durbar*, visited this town. One day, while the Muhammadan was singing, a member of the audience, who wished to gratify the Maharája, exclaimed *Wahwa!*—meaning "Well done!" The artist was much annoyed by this interruption, and requested the Maharája to prohibit inopportune applause. The Maharája complied, and orders were issued that severe punishment would be inflicted upon any person daring to make a noise during a musical performance. Govinda Márár, who was anxious to judge of the Muhammadan's skill, concealed himself in a room adjoining the *durbar* hall. Lost in admiration of the singer's art, Govinda Márár shouted *Wahwa!* at a certain juncture, in defiance of the Maharája's commands.

Govinda Márár was forced to appear before the Maharája, and was ordered to explain his reason for infringing the rules concerning interruptions. The situation threatened to assume an ugly complexion when the Muhammadan intervened, stating that only an expert musician would have chosen the suitable moment, which Govinda Márár had selected, in which to voice his appreciation. Favourably impressed by this testimony to Govinda Márár's scientific knowledge, the Maharája agreed to pardon the culprit, and through his generosity, Márár's position was greatly improved.

Rája Man Singh of Gwalior, mentioned on page 82, was a noted patron of music, and the famous sixteenth century musician, Tán Sen, whose career is sketched on pp. 80 and 81, studied at the academy founded by the Rája. On a recent visit to Gwalior, the author was interested to find that Tán Sen's mausoleum has been restored by the Gwalior Archæological Department. In Europe, where the maintenance of historic buildings is equal in importance to their construction, no particular significance would attach to a similar work of preservation. In India, however—a country where people build, but do not repair—music-lovers owe a special debt of gratitude to the Gwalior Archæological Department, for conserving the monument of one of the greatest musicians India has produced, whose name has come down to posterity as "One of the nine gems of Akbar's Court."

Gwalior State has maintained its musical tradition untarnished for many centuries. His Highness the late Maharája of Gwalior extended his patronage to the All-India Music Conferences, and several artists from the Madho Music School of Gwalior have contributed to the Conference programmes.

Panchpakesa Bhagvatar, to whom reference is made on pp. 2 and 101, as an interpreter of the Rámáyana, died on May 15, 1925, and he is still mourned by all who had the privilege of attending his recitals. He was practically self-taught, but genius will out. Although he did not devote himself to his art until he was about twenty-five years of age, and commenced his public career some two years later, his dynamic skill as a singer soon earned for him tremendous popularity. He gave his performances in Tamil and Telugu, interspersed with quotations in Maráthí and Sanskrit.

Probably Indian audiences are the most appreciative and emotional in the world. They are more concerned with the song than the singer, and concentrate so completely on the work interpreted, that they establish a wondrous bond of sympathy between themselves and the performer. In Indian music, the art of the listener equals in importance the skill of the interpretative artist. In certain Indian cities, it has even been considered necessary to limit public performances of Tyágarája's songs to one per week, as the authorities have found that workmen are ready to spend the whole of their earnings on musical entertainments, instead of purchasing the necessaries of life.

Allusion is made on page 95 to the relation of gipsy songs to Indian music. The connection of the gipsies with India is an interesting ethnological problem. In 1787, an English translation of Grellmann's "Historischer Versuch über die Zigeuner" ("Historical Enquiry concerning the Gipsies") appeared in London. Grellmann identified the gipsies with the Indian *Súdras*, and furnished an extensive vocabulary showing the similarity between the gipsy and Hindustani words. He wrote: "What is further asserted of the young gipsy girls rambling about with their fathers, who are musicians, and dancing . . . . to divert any person who is willing to give them a small gratuity for it, is likewise quite Indian." John Hoyland, in his "Historical Survey of the Customs, Habits and Present State of the Gipsies," York, 1816, supported Grellmann's theories, and cited the opinion of Brand respecting the Eastern origin of the gipsies. Brand remarked: "The gipsies, as it should seem from some striking proofs derived from their language, were, originally, from Hindustan, where they are supposed to have been of the lowest class of Indians, named *Pariahs*, or, as they are called in Hindustan, *Súdras*. They are thought to have emigrated about 1408 or 1409 A.D." In the middle of the nineteenth century, Sir Henry Rawlinson suggested that the gipsies of Europe were descended from the *Lúris*, described by the famous Persian poet, Firdousi (circa 941-1020 A.D.), as minstrels, who were imported into Persia, from India, about 420 A.D.

The *naubat khána*, mentioned on page 84, is one of the most remarkable institutions of Indian music. The effect produced by the bands stationed over the gateways of cities, palaces and shrines is peculiarly impressive when the gateway is situated on a height, for, under these circumstances, the music carries a long distance. Recently, the author climbed the famous Parvati Hill, near Poona, at an early hour and, long before she reached the summit, she distinguished the sounds of the *naubat* band, located over the entrance to the temple of the goddess. In the still, morning air, heavy with monsoon mists, the traditional music acquired fresh charm, enhanced by a flavour of mystery.

Mention of Tibetan musical instruments has been

made on pp. 93 and 94, because of the close proxim-
ity of Tibet to India. At the Indian Museum, Calcutta,
the magnificent collection of musical instruments
comprises specimens from Tibet, which include a
wind instrument very similar to the bone horn illus-
trated on Plate XIII. Dr. Meerwarth, author of an
excellent "Guide" to the Calcutta collection, commented as follows on this peculiar instrument: "It
is a kind of trumpet made from a human thigh-bone.
The *lamas* of Tibet blow it during their ceremonies.
It has found its way into the cult of Buddhism,
together with many other strange customs from
sources much older and darker than the teachings of
Gautama." The present author was assured that the
Tibetan instrument which she examined was manu-
factured from the bone of an animal, but Dr. Meerwarth's remark gives food for reflection as to the
probable origin of the horn, or trumpet, in question.
The *ra-dong*, an immense trumpet, or horn, is to be
found in nearly every Tibetan monastery. Owing
to its great size, however, it is almost impossible for
curio-hunters to smuggle this instrument, unob-
served, across the Tibetan frontier. Readers interested in the sacred music and dancing of Tibet are
referred to "Lands of the Thunderbolt," by the Earl
of Ronaldshay, from which the following extract is

taken : " At the opening of the service the attention of the deities is invoked by music—a wild appeal on cymbals, horns, conchs and drums, swelling in volume and increasing in tumultuousness as it works up gradually towards a crashing climax. Then follows a prayer intoned in soft, deep cadence by the *lamas* chanting in unison. This method of invoca-ion practised in the monasteries throughout Tibet, is characterised by a tone and rhythm which stamp it indelibly upon the memory. . . . The prayers are punctuated by bursts of sound, the roll of drum and the crash of cymbal, and then again there rises on the air the blare of horns and the wild drone of the *ra-dong*. . . . . With a penetrating crash of music the service came to an end."

It would be an inestimable benefit to Indian art, were the efforts which are being made to raise the standard of Indian music, to be extended to Indian dancing, which has deteriorated sadly since the Vedic period, when it was regarded as an occupation fit for kings and their consorts.

At Brindaban, thirty miles south of Delhi, Krishna, mentioned on pp. 26, 97, 105, 129 and 143, passed much of his youth. Here he played his celestial reed *(bansri)* so entrancingly, that the wild beasts and reptiles gathered round to listen to his music. Here he danced his famous *Rása* dance with the *gopis*, or milkmaids, each of whom is supposed to have composed a *rágini* to delight the god. Surely, it is permissible to hope that in the near future Indian music and dancing may be restored to their high estate in honour of Krishna, the pastoral Apollo of the Hindus.

INDIAN MUSIC IN THE PAST AND PRESENT.

CHAPTER I.

ORIGINS.

THE origins of Indian music are to be found in myth and legend, and the united arts of music, drama and dancing are supposed to have been created by the great Hindu god, Siva, the Rudra, or "God of Roaring Tempests," of the Vedas. The Vedic Index proves that a great variety of string, wind and percussion instruments were in use in primitive times, and the "Rig Veda," which is considered by many scholars to date from about B.C. 1400, was recited, originally, to three tones—a practice which prevails to the present day. The ancient "Sáman" chants are taken principally from the ninth book of the "Rig Veda." Distinctions are made between those verses possessing one melody only and those associated with several airs, and this method of differentiation indicates the very close connection which existed between words and music. The Indo-

2

Aryan elements of music are thought to have originated with the Vedic hymns, and rules for the performance of the "Sáman" chants are recorded in Sanskrit treatises.

The ancient Hindu custom of singing or declaiming the great epics to music is still maintained in Southern India. The interpretation of the whole of the "Mahábhárata," or the "Rámáyana," occupies a long series of performances, and the artists employed are greatly fêted. They receive substantial remuneration, and devote their whole lives to the study of the particular epic which they undertake to render in its entirety. One of the most famous of these singers was Panchpakesa Bhagvatar, who performed the whole of the "Rámáyana" in twenty-four recitals, each of which lasted from three to four hours. He died recently, but the enthusiastic praise of music lovers keeps his memory green. Europeans who attended his entertainments were amazed at the manner in which he held his listeners enthralled. Possibly the most dramatic portion of the "Rámáyana" deals with the rescue of Sita, the wife of Prince Ráma. Sita was captured by Ravana, the demon king of Lanka, or Ceylon, and Ráma regained possession of his wife, and overpowered Ravana, with the assistance of the monkey army of King Sugriva. As Panchpakesa Bhagvatar recited this episode, the rapt attention of the audience denoted that each hearer was engrossed in the story and was entirely oblivious to his surroundings.

Both in the "Mahábhárata" (B.C. 500 to A.D. 200) and the "Rámáyana" (B.C. 400 to A.D. 200) frequent reference is made to music, and it is inferred that the art must have reached an advanced stage of development during the centuries when these monumental works were created. In "The Indian Empire,"* Sir William Wilson Hunter remarked that: "A regular system of notation had been worked out before the age of Pánini (B.C. 350), and the seven notes were designated by their initial letters. This notation passed from the Bráhmans through the Persians to Arabia, and was thence introduced into European music by Guido d'Arezzo at the beginning of the eleventh century. . . . . Hindu music, after a period of excessive elaboration, sank under the Muhammadans into a state of arrested development. Of the thirty-six chief musicians in Akbar's time (A.D. 1556-1605) only five were Hindus."

An early and important work in which the theory of music is explained in detail is the "Nátya Sástra," by the sage, Bharata, who is regarded as the founder

---

* "The Indian Empire," by Sir William Wilson Hunter. London, W. H. Allen and Co., 1893 (third edition).

of the present system of Indian music. Some scholars assign it to the first century after Christ, and others to a later period, either to the fourth or to the sixth century. In 1919 a very rare manuscript dealing with music was discovered at Gadwal, the capital of an ancient Hindu state now incorporated in the dominions of H.E.H. the Nizam of Hyderabad. Nárada, the author of this manuscript, which is known as the "Sangíta Makaranda," is believed to have lived between the seventh and eleventh centuries, and his work is one of the very few Sanskrit treatises on music which have been published. Through the intervention of the Resident of Hyderabad, the Hon. Sir Stuart Fraser, K.C.S.I., C.I.E., and Mr. M. A. N. A. Hydari, now Nawab Hydar Nawaz Jung Bahadur, H.H. the Raja Saheb of Gadwal very kindly lent the manuscript to Mr. R. A. K. Shástry, an official employed upon Sanskrit research work by the Baroda Central Library. The valuable document was edited and published under the auspices of H.H. the Maharaja Gáekwár of Baroda, and has proved a most valuable contribution to the history of Indian music.

Another early musician was Jayadeva, the author of the "Gíta Govinda," or "Divine Herdsman," who lived at the end of the twelfth century. His work has been classified as a Sanskrit "Song of Solomon," and has been translated into English by Sir Edwin Arnold, under the title of "The Indian Song of Songs."

Jayadeva was both author and singer, and furnished information respecting the time (*tāla*) and the *rága* or "melody mode" associated with each song. An annual festival to celebrate his memory is held each year at Kendulá, Bengal, Jayadeva's birthplace.

Sárngadeva, another early writer on music, lived at Daulatabad, formerly Deogiri, in the north of H.E.H. the Nizam's dominions. Sárngadeva's "Sangíta Ratnákera" dates from the thirteenth century, and in it he enumerated the twenty-two intervals of the octave as follows:

1.	Tivra	
2.	Kumadvati	Shadja or Sa
3.	Mandá	
4.	Chandovati	
5.	Dayávati	
6.	Ranjaní	Rishaba or Ri
7.	Raktiká	
8.	Rudri	Gándhára or Ga
9.	Krodhá	
10.	Vajriká	
11.	Prasárini	Madhyama or Ma
12.	Prití	
13.	Májaní	

14.	Kshiti	
15.	Raktá	
16.	Sandípa	Pañchama or Pa
17.	Alápi	
18.	Madanti	
19.	Róhini	Dhaivata or Dha
20.	Ramyá	
21.	Vugrá	Nisháda or Ni.
22.	Kshóbini	

The list is included in Captain C. R. Day's "The Music and Musical Instruments of Southern India and the Deccan," London, 1891, an excellent book of reference, now out of print. Day remarked that the list was well known, but that the names have been varied by different authorities. In Hindu mythology the seven principal notes were associated with the cries of animals and birds, and were classified as follows: *Shadja (Sa)*, the cry of the peacock; *Rishaba (Ri)*, the sound made by the cow when calling her calf; *Gándhára (Ga)*, the bleat óf the goat; *Madhyama (Ma)*, the cry of the heron and the tonic of nature; *Pañchama (Pa)*, the note of the cuckoo or *kókila*, the Indian nightingale; *Dhaivata (Dha)*, the neighing of the horse; *Nishada (Ni)*, the trumpeting of an elephant.

The natural form of the notes is known as *prakrita* or *śuddha*, and the chromatics are called *vikrita*.

The latter may be *tívra*, sharp, or *komal*, flat, or *atitívra*, very sharp, or *atikomala*, very flat.

The Hindus are almost unanimous in their praise of music, whereas the Muhammadans disagree as to its merits. Some Muslims consider the art to be an incentive to evil-doing, and regard professional musicians with contempt. Many Muhammadan rulers, however, encouraged the performance of fine music. Akbar, the founder of the Mughal Empire (1556-1605), maintained a large staff of musicians at his court, and in Vol. I of the "Ain-i-Akbari," translated from the original Persian into English by H. Blochmann, the following passage occurs: "His Majesty pays much attention to music, and is the patron of all who practise this enchanting art. There are numerous musicians at court, Hindus, Irani, Turanis, Kashmíris, both men and women. The court musicians are arranged in seven divisions, one for each day in the week." Then follows a list of the thirty-six principal musicians, including singers and performers on the *bín* or *viná*, the most noted of Indian string instruments; the *tambúra*, another popular string instrument; the *qanún*, the Indian dulcimer, of Persian origin; the flute, etc.

When Aurangzeb, the sixth Mughal Emperor of India, ascended the throne in A.D. 1658, he openly evinced his disapproval of music, and many authorities cite the following account of his treatment of the art. The Emperor was in the habit of showing himself every day at a window of his palace, and on one occasion he remarked that several court musicians were stationed outside with a bier, and were performing funeral dirges. He made enquiries as to what was taking place, and the musicians replied that melody was dead, and that they were taking the corpse to be buried. "Very well," replied the Emperor, "make the grave deep, so that neither voice nor echo can proceed from it." Despite his severity and Puritanical tendencies, however, Aurangzeb maintained dancing-girls and singers for the entertainment of his wives and daughters. In his "Storia do Mogor,"* the Italian adventurer and chronicler, Niccolao Manucci, who resided in India from about 1656 to 1717, furnished a list of the superintendents of the dancers and singers at the Mughal court. They were known by such fanciful names as "Gazelle-eyed," "Ruby," "Diamond," "Rose-visaged," etc.

The division of the octave into twelve semitones is superseding the use of twenty-two *śrutis*, or microtones. The modern system was foreshadowed in the

---

* "Storia do Mogor," by Niccolao Manucci. London, John Murray, 1906-1908 (four vols.), translated by William Irvine.

"Sangíta Darpana," or "Mirror of Music," written about A.D. 1625, in which it is stated that there are seven pure tones and twelve impure tones. With the *śrutis*, or quarter tones, were formed the three *grámas*, the *Shadja gráma*, the *Gándhára gráma*, and the *Madhyama gráma*. The *Gándhára gráma* is said to have been lost, but the distribution of the intervals in the other *grámas* was as follows:

Shadja Gráma.

Sa	Ri	Ga	Ma	Pa	Dha	Ni
1 2 3 4	1 2 3	1 2	1 2 3 4	1 2 3 4	1 2 3	1 2
Major tone	Minor tone	Semitone	Major tone	Major tone	Minor tone	Semitone

Madhyama Gráma.

Sa	Ri	Ga	Ma	Pa	Dha	Ni
1 2 3 4	1 2 3	1 2	1 2 3 4	1 2 3	1 2 3 4	1 2
Major tone	Minor tone	Semitone	Major tone	Minor tone	Major tone	Semitone

The term *gráma* gradually fell into disuse, and was replaced by *rága*, implying an arrangement of sounds. *Rágas* may be termed "melody modes," for they consist of certain successions of notes within the octave associated with particular sentiments, and they constitute the basis of Hindu melody. Although all scales now commence from a common tonic, namely, *Sa*, traces of the ancient *grámas* are still to be found in many *rága* forms. There is a wide diversity between the classification of *rágas* in the northern or Hindustani system, and in the southern or Carnatic system. By the Hindustani method *rágas* are divided into six male, or principal, *rágas*, each one of which has five or six wives, or *ráginís*— secondary *rágas*, whilst their children, or *putras*, are known as derivative *rágas*. The Carnatic classification establishes seventy-two root *rágas* formed by variations of the order of the seven notes of the gamut, ascending and descending. *Rágas* have been derived chiefly from tribal songs, poetic works, devotional songs and scientific compositions. About the end of the eighteenth century, Sir William Jones wrote as follows respecting the *rágas* : "Every branch of knowledge in this country has been embellished by poetical fables, and the inventive talents of the Greeks never suggested a more charming allegory than the lovely families of the six *rágas* . . . . each of whom is a genius or demi-god, wedded to five *ráginís* or nymphs, and father of eight little genii, called his *putras* or sons."

The laws respecting the seasons at which certain *rágas* may be performed are still closely observed, and it would be considered a heinous offence for a musician to perform an evening *rága* in the morning, or vice versa. He would be severely censured also, were he to commit any other error respecting the periods associated with certain *rágas*. A modern

musician from Southern India furnished the following list of the periods into which the twenty-four
hours may be divided. The divisions are not identical with those cited by many Indian authorities,
for there seems to be no hard and fast rule amongst
performers as to the exact duration of each period.

First Period		6 to 8.30 a.m.
Second	„	8.30 to 11 a.m.
Third	„	11 a.m. to 1.30 p.m.
Fourth	„	1.30 to 4 p.m.
Fifth	„	4 to 6 p.m.
Sixth	„	6 to 9 p.m.
Seventh	„	9 p.m. to 1 a.m.
Eighth	„	1 a.m. to 3 a.m.
Ninth	„	3 a.m. to 6 a.m.

Certain *rágas* are associated with natural phenomena. The *Megh Mallar rága*, for instance, is supposed to produce rain and, on one occasion, a
dancing-girl of Bengal is said to have saved the
crops in a time of drought, by singing this *rága* and
causing rain to fall immediately. Superstitious folk
in the Deccan still believe in the power of this *rága*,
but either it must have lost its efficacy, or no musician exists at the present day who can perform it
satisfactorily, for there has been a shortage of water
in many parts of this area for the past seven years.

A story is extant respecting the Emperor Akbar, who commanded the famous singer, Naik Gopāl, to perform *rága Dípak*, knowing this rága to be related to fire. Naik Gopāl did his utmost to evade fulfilling tne Emperor's commands, but Akbar was adamant. Accordingly, the unfortunate musician took the precaution of standing in the river Jumna before commencing his song, but all in vain—the heat of the water increased as he continued his performance until flames burst from his body and destroyed him.

In the ancient theory of Indian music three important notes were designated, namely, the *graha*, or starting note, the *amśa*, or predominant note, and the *nyása*, or final note of the *rága*. To-day importance centres solely round the *amśa* or *vádí*, known as "the soul of the *rága*." The example below illustrates the *Bhairáva rága* of the north, which is known in the south as the *Máyámálavagaula rága*. It is associated with dawn, and is of a reverent and quiet nature. Flattened *dha* is the *amśa*. This *rága* is the foundation of many folk-songs and melodies sung by the peasants when at work. On a recent visit to the sacred river Godavari, where a railway bridge was in process of construction, within the confines of Hyderabad state, the author was interested to note that this *rága* seemed to form the

basis of the work-song of the coolies as they hauled
machinery and building materials to the river bank.

Ex. 1.

Bhairāva Rāga, or Māyāmālavagaula Rāga.

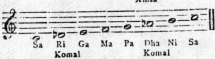

Sa   Ri   Ga   Ma   Pa   Dha   Ni   Sa
     Komal   Komal

The Rev. H. A. Popley includes a remarkably
comprehensive collection of specimen *rágas* in his
small volume, "The Music of India" (Calcutta, Association Press, 1921). He is one of the few European musicians who possess practical as well as
theoretical knowledge of Indian music, and his work
should be perused by all serious students anxious
to gain insight into the vocal and instrumental re-
sources of the vast Indian empire.

CHAPTER II.

"RAGMALA," or the art of *rága* pictures, forms an interesting supplement to *rága* music, and is described by Lord Ronaldshay in "The Heart of Aryávarta" (London, Constable, 1925), as follows: "This practice of weaving music and painting into a single composite whole provides us with a striking example of the intention claimed by the Indian for Indian art, namely, that of giving expression to the idea which lies behind the appearance of things—of making manifest the abstract; for it is, surely, ideas only and not objects, such as persons or things, that lend themselves to reproduction in two such different forms of artistic expression as music and painting."

It is possible to obtain *ríga* pictures in many Indian cities, but the warning expressed by Sir William Jones in his article, "On the Antiquity of the Indian Zodiac," respecting Indian drawings in general, is applicable, in particular, to *rágmala*. Sir

William Jones wrote: "Whenever the Indian drawing differs from the memorial verse in the *Retna-
mála*, I have preferred the authority of the writer
to that of the painter, who has drawn some terres-
trial things with so little similitude, that we must
not rely implicitly on his representation of objects."
Some fine specimens of *rága* paintings are preserved
in the Johnson Collection at the India Office, London, and in his "Treatise on the Music of Hindustan," included in "Hindu Music from Various
Authors," compiled and published by Raja. Comm.
Sourindro Mohun Tagore (Calcutta, 1882, now out
of print), Captain Augustus Willard* gives some
graphic descriptions of these visualised melodies.
He refers to the picture of the *Megh rága*,
which is associated with rain (see page 11):
"This *rág* is represented of a dark complexion, his
hair is tied in a knot on the crown of his head, and
in his hand he balances a sharp-edged sword." *Rága
Dípak* (mentioned in page 12) is depicted frequently with a flaming countenance to indicate his
relation to fire. He rides a savage elephant and is
accompanied by a large number of females. Mr.
C. R. Sreenivas Iyengar, one of the most noted musi-

* Captain Augustus Willard commanded the troops in the
service of H.H. the Nawab of Banda, about the year 1834.

cal authorities in Southern India, has been in correspondence with the author respecting *rágmala*, and he is of opinion "that each classic *rága* has a pen portrait of it in the *Dhyana-śloka* attached to it. That is the verse depicting the goddess of that *rága*, who, if approached and prayed to in the proper way, confers on the votary, mastery of that *rága*."

In his "Universal History of Music" (Calcutta, 1896, now out of print), Raja Sir Sourindro Mohun Tagore alluded to the colour scheme which Sanskrit experts have associated with music: "According to Sanskrit authorities the seven notes are respectively represented by the following colours: black, tawny, golden, white, yellow, purple and green, resembling very nearly those mentioned in Field's 'Chromatics.' . . . . The Sanskrit authorities divide the notes into castes, C, F and G (each of which contains four *śrutis*) being Bráhmanas; D and A (each having three *śrutis*) being Kshatriyas; E and B (having two *śrutis* each) being Vaisyas; and the sharps and flats being Súdras (or pariahs, these having lost caste, so to speak, by the relative values of the notes they represented being affected). This grouping furnishes the key to the combination that should be resorted to in setting a musical piece to harmony. The arrangement of the colours, too, furnishes an important guide in the arrangement of chords."

In ancient India the Bráhmans, or priests, constituted the highest caste, and claimed supremacy alike over king and people, and in modern times they are still the most venerated members of society. The Kshattriyas surrounded the king or chief, and were soldiers. The ancient Sanskrit names of "Kshattriya," "Rájanya" and "Rájbansi" signified "connected with the royal line," hence the derivation of the modern "Rájput," meaning "of royal descent." The Vaisyas were the agriculturists, whereas the Súdras, descendants of the aboriginal tribes conquered by the Aryans, were treated as slaves.

Extract from Sir William Wilson Hunter's "The Indian Empire" (W. H. Allen and Co., 1893). "The Aryans on the Ganges, in the 'Middle Land,' thus found themselves divided into three classes : first, the priests, or Bráhmans; second, the warriors and king's companions, called in ancient times Kshattriyas, at the present day Rájputs ; third, the husbandmen, or agricultural settlers, who retained the old name of Vaisyas, from the root *vis*, which in the Vedic period had included the whole 'people.' These three classes gradually became separate castes ; intermarriage between them was forbidden, and each kept more and more strictly to its hereditary employment. *But they were all recog-*

3

nised as belonging to the 'Twice-born' or Aryan race; they were all present at the great national sacrifices; and all worshipped the same Bright Gods.

"Beneath them was a fourth or servile class, called Súdras, the remnants of the vanished aboriginal tribes whose lives had been spared. These were 'the slave-bands of black descent,' the Dásas of the Veda. They were distinguished from their 'Twice-born' Aryan conquerors as being only 'Once-born,' and by many contemptuous epithets. They were not allowed to be present at the great national sacrifices, or at the feasts which followed them. They could never rise out of their servile condition; and to them was assigned the severest toil in the fields, and all the hard and dirty work of the village community."

Extract from "India: A Bird's Eye View," by the Earl of Ronaldshay (Constable and Co., 1924): "It is often popularly supposed that the term caste refers to the four great divisions into which, as we learn from the ancient Sanskrit texts of a semi-priestly and semi-legal character, the immigrant Aryan people was separated; that is to say, the Bráhmans or priesthood, the Kshattriya or military class, the Vaisya or husbandmen, and the Súdra or lower orders, whose function it was to serve the members of the first three. These were certainly more or less definite classes—as they are to this day—which were evolved by a process of elaboration from the two great groups of people who met on the soil of India as a result of the incursions from the north-west, to which reference has been made, namely, the immigrant Aryans and the aboriginal inhabitants whom they found already in possession of the land. The former were sharply divided from the latter in that they alone were admitted to the reading of the Vedas and to participation in the religious ceremonies associated therewith. They were the true Aryans, and to this day the members of the three classes in question are known as the twice-born, from the fact that they are initiated into the ceremonial of the ancient religion and invested with the sacred thread—the outward and visible sign of their second or spiritual birth."

The use of grace notes is a conspicuous feature of Indian music. In "Rágavibodha," a treatise on music by the Sanskrit authority, Somanátha, written about A.D. 1609, fifty examples of *gamaka*, grace, are given in various *rágas*, and it is stated that "a melody devoid of embellishments is like a moonless night, a river without water, a creeper without flowers, or a woman without a garment." With the modern tendency to divide the octaves into twelve semitones, microtones are freely employed as embellishments. There are about nineteen varieties of *gamaka* which assume importance in Hindu melody, and lend dignity and character such as harmony supplies in European music. One of the most frequent ornaments is the *Humpitam* or appoggiatura (Ex. 2).

Ex. 2.
Humpitam

played

This grace adds vigour to the principal note, and is much employed in singing. Full *humpitam* is heard when the grace-note is more than a semitone below the principal note. *Ahata* occurs when the grace is a semitone only above the principal note.

The *Andolitam* is another popular form of *gamaka* (Ex. 3).

Ex. 3.
Andolitam

The *andolitam* produces a pleasant, lilting or swinging effect.

Trills, tremolo passages, staccato notes and *Linum* or sliding notes, introduce welcome variation into phrases which might become monotonous, owing to

frequent repetition, if performed without *gamaka*.
Grace emphasises the important notes of the *rága*,
and figures largely for this purpose in the *Áláp*,
or prelude, with which a vocalist prefaces the performance of the actual melody. When utilised in
this manner grace is sometimes known as *múrchana*.
The *áláp* is taken at a slow pace to enable the
listeners to become familiar with the characteristics
of the tune, and to assist the vocalist or instrumentalist to enter into the spirit of the composition
The value of the *áláp* is indisputable, but it is
apt to become wearisome to Europeans. In the
East, time is of no account, and a conscientious
musician will devote an hour or more to the prelim-
inary test of the *áláp*, before commencing his
actual solo. A feature of Indian music which is
confusing at the outset to European ears is the constant employment of *portamento*. In his illumin-
ating article entitled "Indian Music," reprinted from
the 1917 April number of the New York publication, "The Musical Quarterly," Ananda Coomaraswamy wrote: "Equally distinctive is the constant
portamento. In India it is far more the interval
than the note that is sung or played, and we recognise accordingly a continuity of sound : by contrast
with this, the European song, which is vertically
divided by the harmonic interest, and the nature of

the keyed instruments which are heard with the voice, seems to unaccustomed Indian ears to be 'full of holes.'"

The outstanding categories of melodies in use in Northern and Southern India are known as *Dhurpad* and *Khyál* in the north, and as *Kirtana* and *Kriti* in the south. The individual sections of the *kirtana* or *dhurpad* are more clearly defined than those of the *kriti*. In his "Treatise on the Music of Hindustan," mentioned on page 15, Willard noted a few distinctive traits of Hindu melodies: "1. Hindustani melodies are short, lengthened by repetition and variations. 2. They all partake of the nature of what is denominated by us 'Rondo,' the piece being invariably concluded with the first strain, and sometimes with the first bar, or at least with the first note of that bar. 3. A bar, or measure, or a certain number of measures, are frequently repeated, with slight variations, almost *ad lib.* 4. There is as much liberty allowed with respect to pauses, which may be lengthened at pleasure, provided the time be not disturbed."

The various sections of the melodies are known in the south as *Pallavi*, *Anupallavi* and *Charanam*, and in the north as *Astái*, *Antara*, *Sañchári* and *Abhog*. The *pallavi*, or *astái*, contains the main subject, and usually possesses a well-defined rhythm. In the *anupallavi* or *antara*, the second subject is introduced, and serves as an answer to the refrain of the *pallavi*. Phrases from both sections are employed in the *charanam* (*sañchári*). The *charanam* affords much scope for the interpolation of elaborate ornamentation, as the rhythm is less definitely punctuated than in the *pallavi* and *anupallavi*. The *ábhog* of the north is a *coda*, into which the composer frequently inserts his own name.

Rhythm is very complicated in Indian music, but about twelve varieties only are in general use, although Sárngadeva specified one hundred and twenty categories. In his "Music of Hindustan" (published in 1914 by the Oxford University Press), which has been classified as "the only thoroughly scientific treatise on the subject by an expert in western music, and a keen student of Indian music," Fox Strangways wrote: "In order that rhythm, an articulation of the infinite variety of sounds, may be upon some regular plan, the plan must have some recognisable unit of measurement. India takes the short note and gives it for a particular rhythm a certain value as opposed to the long; Europe takes the stressed note and gives it in a particular rhythm a certain frequency as against the unstressed, and graduates its force. We find the unity of the rhythm in the recurrent bar (which is always in duple or triple time, just as our two melodic modes are either major or minor) and have to look elsewhere for the variety; they find variety in the *vibhág* (bar), whose constitution is, as we have seen, extremely various, and must look elsewhere for unity. Both of us find what we want in the larger spaces of time; they find unity in the *ávard* (section), we find variety in the sections."* There is a very close connection between the metre of verse and the rhythm of music in India, for the musical measure has been affected by the structure of the language and by the prosody. The Hindustani and Carnatic systems of *Tála* (time), have many points of resemblance, and were both derived from poetic metre. Accent is unknown in Indian verse, and great attention is paid to the duration of the syllables, with the result that the rhythm of music has been influenced by the versification.

Time may be slow, moderate and quick, *Vilamba*, *Madhya* and *Drita*, and the subdivisions include duple, triple, quintuple, septuple and nonuple measures. The last-mentioned is seldom employed. A bar containing one group of units or *Mátras*, produces a more subtle emotional effect than one

---

* The English words in brackets have been added to elucidate the meaning.—E. R.

THE MRDANGA

Plate II.
THE TABLA.

(*See the description of the* mrdanga *and* tabla *on pages* 28 *and* 29.)

Plate III.

Manahar Barve with his Sárangí.

(See the description of the sárangí on page 30 and the reference to Manahar Barve's sárangí on page 145.)

containing two or three groups of notes. A pecu-
liarity of Indian rhythm is the *Chápu Tála*, in
which the contents of a whole bar constitute one
group of *mátras*. The following examples include specimens of the most common of these measures, namely, the *Trisra Játi*, in $\frac{3}{16}$ time, and the
Misra Játi, in $\frac{7}{16}$ time. The latter might be termed
the national rhythm of Southern India, and reflects
the predilection of the people for the number seven.
Its progression might be expressed in notes of increasing value, as under (Ex. 4a).

Ex. 4a.

Misra Játi in notes of increasing value.

Ex. 4. Cháputâlas.*

Trisra Játi

Khanda Játi

---

* These and more extensive examples of *Cháputâlas* are
contained in "Oriental Music in European Notation," by
Mr. Chinnaswami Mudaliyar, Madras, 1893, a rare work
dealing with Carnatic music.

Misra Jāti

Sankīrna Jāti

Captain Day observed : * " True triple time, curiously enough, is of the rarest, but there is a time, the accentuation of which is upon the first and second beat, which may be said to be a kind of triple time." This hybrid measure is a mixture of duple and common time, which is frequently employed in love songs to lend an impassioned character to the music.

Krishna, the pastoral incarnation of Vishnu, is represented frequently playing the flute, and he is the hero of innumerable love songs. He is regarded as an irresistible enchanter, and the tales of his amorous adventures delight young and old alike. Music plays an important part in the mystery play, based on the loves of Krishna and his bride, Rádhá, described by Sir William Wilson

---

* " The Music and Musical Instruments of Southern India and the Deccan."

Hunter as: "that woodland pastoral redolent of a wild-flower aroma as ethereal as the legend of Psyche and Cupid." Many of the Indian love songs heard to-day are a product of a bygone age, and in them it is not unusual for the woman to be represented as seeking the man. Doubtless this attitude is attributable to the polygamous customs formerly in vogue, when a woman's chief occupation was to capture her husband's affection or to chain a lover to her side, despite the impediments of mother-in-law and other female relations, with whom she shared her husband's home.

In the Appendix, a reprint is given of the section of Captain Willard's treatise entitled "Of the Peculiarities of Manners and Customs in Hindustan to which Allusions are made in their Song."

Maráthá love songs, however, are full of incident, consequent upon the exploits of this warlike Hindu tribe, and their disputes with the English and the Muhammadans. The spring season in particular is associated with love-making in India. Swinging is a favourite class of entertainment at this period, and special songs are composed to celebrate this diversion. They are of a rhythmic character, and are dedicated to Krishna's wife, who is the patroness of swinging.

Indian drummers devote much study to acquiring

rhythmic independence of each hand and, as Fox Strangways mentioned in his "Music of Hindustan": "Indian drumming, then, varies the quality rather than the quantity of the tone. It practically ignores accent for its own sake. Such accent as there is on the first of the bar is due to the fact that two rhythms diverge from that point and converge at the beginning of the next or a later bar. It is the accent induced by the juxtaposition of opposing metres . . . . that pleases the Indian; not the accent, which is sought for its own sake as a means of contrast."

The drum occupies an important position in Hindu myth and legend, and in India the varieties of this instrument are legion. The *mrdanga* is considered generally to be the most ancient Indian drum. The two heads are covered with parchment and are tuned by means of braces. A mixture of flour and water is frequently applied to one head to increase the resonance, and the plaster is removed with care after each performance, whereas on the other drum head "the eye," as it is sometimes called, consisting of boiled rice, dust and juice, is permanent. Similar pastes are applied to the *tabla*, or pair of drums, which has been likened in appearance to a pair of cups, one of large and one of medium size. Professor Abdul Karim, of Poona, invented recently a collection of *tablas* tuned to the notes of the scale and known as the *tabala tarang*. The *dhol*, or wedding drum, is not unlike the *mṛdangā*, but it is played usually with sticks instead of with the fingers, and produces a hollow sound. It is heard incessantly during the Hindu wedding season—a period dependent upon the favourable position of certain stars

A curious attempt to unite Indian music with European drama occurred recently at the court of an Indian Mahará̇ja, when his subjects performed a Hindu adaptation of "Measure for Measure." There was so much singing that many scenes were suggestive of comic opera rather than of legitimate drama, and portions of the music, such as the duets between Isabella and Claudio, were really dramatic. As is customary in India, the women's rôles were played by men, and the actors who represented the weaker sex employed a peculiar falsetto when singing which was not unpleasant. The orchestra consisted of a harmonium supported by a pair of *tabla*, which provided a rhythmic accompaniment to the comic scenes and linked up the episodes. Other festivities at this same Indian court included the celebration of a number of Hindu marriages. The gaieties, *tamáshas*, connected with each wedding lasted several days, and no expense was spared in engaging singing and dancing girls, who came specially from Delhi to entertain the Maharája and his guests. Each girl was assisted by three instrumentalists, two of whom played on the *sárangí*, or Indian violin, whilst the third provided the inevitable *tabla* accompaniment. The drummers showed great skill in the employment of curious rhythmic devices, and really constituted the backbone of the entertainment, as the singers and dancers relied upon them to keep time. The *sárangís* used were of various sizes, some being about two feet in height, whereas others were considerably larger. In shape these instruments are reminiscent of the guitar, and usually have four strings, three of gut and one of brass. Formerly, Hindus favoured the exclusive use of metal strings to obviate the risk of employing gut made from the intestines of the cow, their sacred animal, but gut strings are to be found on many *sárangís* at the present day. The *sárangí* is popular both with professionals and amateurs, and lends itself to all categories of grace notes, as the stopping is produced by placing the fingers against the sides of the strings instead of pressing upon them. The belly is covered with parchment, beneath which a support is placed for the bridge. The four strings are tuned to Sa, Pa, Sa, Ga, or Sa, Ma (C, G, C, E, or C, F), and most *sárangís* have a number of sympathetic understrings.

The larger instruments employed by the accompanists of the dancing girls possessed twenty-two understrings, and the tone produced was rich and mellow.

The girls commenced their performance during the course of a Gargantuan banquet, at which no less than seventy kinds of comestibles were served to the men guests. The only females present were the entertainers and the author, as the Indian ladies of the establishment and their friends were in *parda*, and remained hidden in the *zenana*. The artists possessed most enviable powers of concentration, and remained engrossed in their work, despite the perpetual movement of servants, attendants and other satellites who ministered to the wants of the Maharája and his suite. Before each song the vocalists ran through the melody with the principal *sárangi* players, who stood close beside them, and during the performance the soloists gave their orders to the instrumentalists. Most of the lyrics were of an amorous nature, as befitted the character of the festivities, and the music continued for about six hours. At the close of the repast the author was ushered into the *zenana* by the bridegroom, and was entertained by the ladies, who sang to their own harmonium accompaniment. Their voices were melodious, but the instrument was raucous and out-of-tune, and obliter-

ated the finenesses of their vocalisation. Unfortunately the harmonium has acquired great popularity
throughout India, although it has little to recommend it. It is to be regretted, however, that the interesting instrument designed by Mr. H. Keatley
Moore and tuned in the twenty-two *śrutis*, which was
patented by Messrs. Moore and Moore, is no longer
on the market, for the ordinary harmonium, beloved
of Hindus and Muhammadans alike, detracts from
the enjoyment of all sensitive listeners

THE SOUTHERN VINÁ.

The Southern *viná* shown in the photograph came from Tanjore. It was of medium size, being about three and a half feet in length, and was priced at seventy rupees, as the ivory ornamentation of the instrument was simple. Larger and more elaborately decorated instruments realise considerable sums of money, as they are greatly admired. The first two strings of the Southern *viná* are usually of brass and the remaining five, including the three side strings, are of steel. The *viná* here represented was tuned in the following manner, which was described by the performer as Pa Sa, Pa Sa, Sa Pa Sa.

The Southern *viná* differs somewhat both in construction and tuning from the bin (been) or *viná* of the North described by Francis Fowke (see page 34). It will be noticed that the *viná* of the South has only one gourd, and a bowl hollowed out of one piece of wood.

p. 49

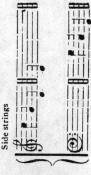

Side strings

Fingerboard

p. 38

Plate V.

SOUTHERN VÍNÁ PLAYER.

Court Musician to the Maharája of Vizianagram
The víná was presented by the Maharájá.

(Reproduced by kind permission of Mrs. C. R. Marsh.)

CHAPTER III.

THE VÍNÁ AND SOME OTHER INSTRUMENTS.

THE finest string instrument of India is the *víná*, sometimes known as the *bin*. The southern *víná* is of graceful appearance, consisting of a large bowl hollowed out of one piece of wood, upon which the bridge is placed and furnished with a number of sounding holes. The southern *víná* is seen occasionally in England, and is recognisable by the curved neck and the gourd, which increases the volume of tone and serves as a rest for the instrument. In shape the *víná* is supposed to represent the body of the goddess Parvati, by reason of the curved neck, the gourds or breasts, and the frets or bracelets. A very interesting description of the *bin* or Northern *víná* was contributed by Francis Fowke to Volume I of "Asiatic Researches," and was reproduced by Raja Comm. Sourindro Mohun Tagore, in his "Hindu Music from Various Authors." Fowke wrote: "The *bin* (been)

4

is a fretted instrument of the guitar kind.
The fingerboard is 21¾ inches long. A little beyond
each end of the fingerboard are two large gourds,
and beyond these are the pegs and tail-piece which
hold the wires. The whole length of the instrument
is 3 feet 7 inches. The first gourd is fixed at 10 inches
from the top, and the second is about 2 feet 11½
inches. The gourds are very large, about 14 inches
diameter, and have a round piece cut out of the
bottom, about 5 inches diameter. The fingerboard is
about 2 inches wide. The wires are seven in number, and consist of two steel ones, very close together,
in the right side; four brass ones on the fingerboard;
and one brass one on the left side. They are tuned
in the following manner (Ex. 5).

Ex. 5.

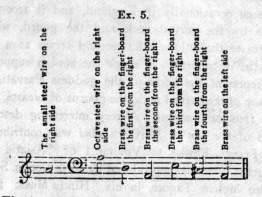

"The great singularity of this instrument is the

height of the frets; that nearest the nut is $1\frac{1}{8}$ inch, and that at the other extremity about $\frac{7}{8}$ of an inch, and the decrease is pretty gradual. By this means the finger never touches the fingerboard itself. The frets are fixed on with wax by the performer himself, which he does entirely by ear. . . . . Any little difference is easily corrected by the pressure of the finger. Indeed, the performers are fond, on any note that is at all long, of pressing the string very hard and letting it return immediately to its natural tension, which produces a sound something like the close shake on the violin, but not with so agreeable an effect; for it appears sometimes to alter the sound half a tone. . . . . The *bín* (been) is held over the left shoulder, the upper gourd resting on that shoulder, the lower one on the right knee. The frets are stopped with the left hand; the first and second fingers are principally used. . . . The third finger is seldom used, the hand shifting up and down the fingerboard with great rapidity. The fingers of the right hand are used to strike the strings of this hand; the thir finger is never used. The two first fingers strike the wires on the fingerboard, and the little finger strikes the two wires."

Modern *vínás* have as many as twenty-four frets, and some of the finest instruments are made in Tanjore and Mysore. The *vínā* is played with the finger-nails or with a plectrum, and is a popular instrument with ladies in the south, whereas in the north it is used almost exclusively by professional musicians. Rao Saheb Abraham Pandither, of Tanjore, recently constructed a *vínà* which he divided into forty-eight equal parts to the octave.

Many charming legends are extant respecting the *vínà*, and the following story contains a lesson for all musicians suffering from "swollen heads." The monkey god, Hanumán, was exceedingly proud of his great skill as a performer, and Ráma, weary of his boasting, determined to cure him. A certain *rishi*, or sage, a composer of Vedic hymns, converted the seven notes of the octave into beautiful nymphs who passed Hanumán as he played upon the *vínà*. One of the nymphs died as she listened to the monkey god, for she was the embodiment of the note which the conceited deity had murdered. The *rishi* then took up the *vínà*, and the nymph revived as the note was played correctly. Hanumán was ashamed of his folly, and repented of his desire to pose as a great musician. Various versions of this legend are to be found in Indian works dealing with the art of music, but they all point the same moral.

In the Deccan and in Bombay Presidency, it is easier to discover performers on the *sitár*, than *vínà* players, although the *vínà* is regarded as the national instrument of India. The invention of the *sitár* is attributed to Amír Khusru, a famous poet and singer, who was attached to the court of Sultan Alá-ud-Dín Khiljí, of Delhi (1295-1315). The principles of the *sitár* are similar to those of the *vínú*, but the *sitár* is a simpler and more portable instrument, as it has no curved neck nor gourd attachment. There are usually seven strings, five of steel and two of brass, and many *sitárs* are furnished with a large number of sympathetic understrings which vibrate when the principal strings are sounded. As an accompaniment to the voice the *sitár* is a delightfully responsive instrument. Certain Parsi ladies excel in playing on this instrument, and it is most interesting to hear the comic songs which they perform to their own *sitár* accompaniment. These items are suggestive of the English "Songs at the Piano," and several of the artists might be termed "Margaret Coopers of the East," owing to the skill with which they maintain the balance between words and music. The peacock *taush*, so called because the head of the instrument is shaped like a peacock, and the body resembles the tail and supports strings and tuning-pegs, is a curiosity not often heard. One such instrument is preserved at the famous Sikh temple at Nander in the dominions of H.E.H. the Nizam of Hyderabad. Great attention is paid to the music at

Nander, where the singers and instrumentalists are as noted as those at the Golden Temple, Amritsar. They perform at the evening ceremonies, which last from two to three hours, and are stationed in the centre of the Nander temple, near the inner sanctuary containing the tomb of the great Guru Govind, the Sikh leader, who was murdered at Nander a little over two hundred years ago. Singing and chanting are important features of the ritual, and a large number of bells, gongs, cymbals and horns are used. Various huge shells are employed for fanfares and rhythmic accompaniments, and although producing a harsh sound, they are in keeping with the military atmosphere of the temple, which is guarded by armed sepoys, and decorated with votive offerings, consisting of two-edged swords and other warlike implements. The soldiers watch carefully to see that Europeans remain in a small portion of the side veranda, from which they can view the proceedings in the central enclosure, without interfering with the devotions of the faithful.

In Hindu temples, chiefly those of the Lingayet sects, a peculiar form of music is employed known as *karadismêla*, owing to the use of a large kettledrum of this name. Huge gongs are conspicuous at the *Dasahra* festival, dedicated to the memory of ancestors, and, at sunset, Hindu women carry baskets of coloured rice and garlands of flowers to the banks of the rivers, to the accompaniment of these instruments of percussion. On this occasion workmen decorate their tools and worship, do *puja*, to them, whilst the music of cymbals, gongs and harmoniums provides a musical background to their devotions.*

Interesting specimens of Indian music, influenced by contact with Europe, are to be heard in Portuguese India. Although Nova Goa, the capital of Portuguese India, is a stronghold of Roman Catholicism, a large proportion of the inhabitants are Hindu. The Indians have come very closely in touch with the European and semi-European inhabi-

---

* In his "Hindu Manners, Customs and Ceremonies" (translated by H. K. Beauchamp, Oxford University Press, 1897), Abbé Dubois made the following comment respecting the *Dasahra* festival: "The *Dasahra* is likewise the soldiers' feast. Princes and soldiers offer the most solemn sacrifices to the arms which are made use of in battle. Collecting all their weapons together, they call a Bráhman *purohita*, who sprinkles them with *tirtham* (holy water) and converts them into so many divinities by virtue of his *mantrams*. He then makes *puja* to them and retires. Thereupon, amidst the beat of drums, the blare of trumpets and other instruments, a ram is brought in with much pomp and sacrificed in honour of the various weapons of destruction. This ceremony is observed with the greatest solemnity throughout the whole Peninsular, not only by the Hindu princes and soldiers, but also by the Muhammadans."

tants, and this intercourse has affected their music. At Xri Manguexa (Manguexim), in the Portuguese district of Ponda, bells, drums, horns and Indian string instruments are employed in the temple consecrated to Siva worship. The horns are constructed from pieces of brass which can be fitted together to form a long curve; they are known in the south by the Tamil name of *kombu*, meaning horn, and in the north as *śringa*, or *śing*. They are employed extensively at all festivals and processions, and are utilised by village watchmen. Several of the instruments in Manguexim temple are so cumbersome that special push-carts are required to convey them from one part of the building to another, but despite their primitive construction the performers obtain rhythmic and melodic effects suggestive of western compositions.

The sacred ankle-bells of the dancing-girls are heard regularly in the Hindu temples at Goa, and the pleasant modulations of the girls' voices, as they blend with the bells, produce a harmonious combination, refreshing to European ears weary of the strident notes of the conch and the clash of cymbals. No dancer ties on these bells without first holding them to her forehead and uttering a short prayer, for they are the symbols of the profession to which she has been dedicated. "To tie on the bells" has

Plate VI.

MANAHAR BARVE WITH HIS SITÁR.

(See the description of the sitar on page 37, and the reference to Manahar Barve's sitár on page 146.)

Plate VII.

MANAHAR BARVE WITH HIS BURMESE GONGS.

(See the reference to Manahar Barve's Burmese gongs on page 147.)

become a proverb signifying that a person has undertaken some enterprise or duty which cannot be abandoned. In Goa the girls offer flowers to foreign visitors as they leave the temples, and, in consequence, it is easy for the westerner to judge of their manners and appearance at close quarters. Like most temple women, they are clean and educated, their movements are graceful, and their performances are intelligent and artistic.*

---

* In "The Dance of Life" (Constable, 1923), Havelock Ellis wrote: "In India again, the *Devadasis*, or sacred dancing girls, are at once both religious and professional dancers. They are married to gods, they are taught dancing by the Bráhmans, they figure in religious ceremonies, and their dances represent the life of the god they are married to as well as the emotions of love they experience for him. Yet, at the same time, they also give professional performances in the houses of rich private persons who pay for them. It thus comes about that to the foreigner the *Devadasis* scarcely seem very unlike the *Ramedjenis*, the dancers of the street, who are of very different origin, and mimic in their performances the play of merely human passions. The Portuguese conquerors of India called both kinds of dancers indiscriminately *Balheideras* (or dancers), which we have corrupted into *Bayaderes*."

* In 1922, Otto Rothfeld wrote in "Women of India," (Taraporevala and Sons, Bombay): "Besides Tanjore, the old Portuguese possession of Goa and the neighbouring districts bordering on the ocean, where the forests and rocks of the Western Ghauts drop sharply to the rice-lands of the shore, are famous for the excellence of their singers. Here they are known under the name of *Naikins* or 'Ladyships,' and have a position of no little respect.

In 1878 Da Fonseca commented upon the love of music evinced by the Goanese in general, and remarked in his " Historical and Archæological Sketch of Goa," that: "It is a circumstance worthy of notice that the people of Goa, as a rule, possess a peculiar taste for music; but it is only amongst the upper and educated ranks that the principal European musical instruments are in use. The humbler classes still adhere to the national musical instruments, such as *gumbhot*, a quasi-semicircular earthen vessel ending in a small open tube, and covered in the front with a lizard skin; and *madlem*, a cylindrical earthen vessel covered on both ends with the same skin. The former is played with the right hand, and is specially used as an accompaniment to

---

Though they like to trace their origin in their own sayings to those nymphs who in heaven are said to entertain the Gods, the truth is that they are largely recruited from other classes, whose children they purchase or adopt. They live in houses like those of the better-class Hindus, with broad verandahs and large court-yards, in which grows a plant or two of the sacred sweet basil. Their homes are furnished in the plain style of the Hindu householder, with mats and stools and wooden benches and an abundance of copper and brass pots and pans and water vessels. Only they wear a profusion of gold ornaments on head and wrists and fingers, a silver waist-band, and silver rings on their toes, and they make their hair gay with flowers. Their lives are simple and not luxurious; but the days are idled away in the languorous ease of the tropic sea breezes, a land of repose, a lazy land."

the popular country dance of *mando*, and the latter
with both hands." The musical conditions in Goa
have altered very little since the days of Da Fonseca, but this writer's remarks may be supplemented
by a few observations respecting the cult of Portuguese folk-song in Goa. The students sing the
fados (folk-songs) to their own accompaniment
upon the guitarre and Portuguese viola. The only
noticeable distinctions between their renderings and
the interpretations heard in Portugal, are to be found
in the exaggerated syncopation and excessively halt-
ing rhythm adopted by the Goanese. This Asiatic
lethargy, however, has not affected the Goanese or-
chestras devoted to jazz and other modern dance
music, and Indo-Portuguese musicians are in great
demand at balls throughout British India.

CHAPTER IV.

TYÁGARÁJA: THE BEETHOVEN OF INDIAN MUSIC.

EUROPEANS are prone to condemn Indian singing after listening to one or two performances of an inferior standard, at which they have been disgusted with the grimaces and coarse vocalisation of the musicians. The following remarks of the famous writer on India, Meadows Taylor, author of "The Confessions of a Thug," are as applicable to-day as they were in the earlier part of the nineteenth century: "I am bound to state, that very little of the really good or classical music of the Hindus is ever heard by European ears. What is ordinarily played to them is the commonest ballads and love-songs, with modern Persian and Hindustani ditties, sung by ill-instructed screaming dancing women, at crowded native *durbars*, marriages and other ceremonies." Fine vocalists are rare in India, and frequently they hesitate to perform before foreigners who are apt to show their contempt for In-

dian music without endeavouring to understand it.
Pierre Loti responded to the charm of Indian lyrics,
and wrote in "L'Inde (Sans les Anglais)": "These
songs are neither so upsetting nor so sad to us as
those of Mongolia or China. We can understand
them almost completely. They convey to us the
extreme sensitiveness of a humanity which has
drifted far away from us during the course of centuries, but of one which is not radically different
from ours."

Probably the most famous of all modern Indian
composers was Tyágarája, who is said to have composed melodies in every southern *rága*. According
to Indian *pandits*, musicians must possess firm devotion to God and must be pure in mind and body,
for unless they realise the spiritual power of music
they will be unable to gauge the science underlying
their art. The following notes on the life and work
of Tyágarája were translated from information published in Tamil and Telugu, respecting this Beet-
hoven of Indian music. All records prove that
Tyágarája was an idealist who led a saintly existence. He was born in Thiruvalur, in the Tanjore
district, about 1759, and was one of several sons.
His father was a sage well versed in Vedic lore,
from whom the future composer acquired consider-

able knowledge of ancient literature, before devoting himself to the study of singing. In a prodigiously short time Tyágarája's talents were recognised, and he was acknowledged to be one of the finest vocalists in the south of India. He then became the disciple of a *swámi*—a term of respect applied to a man of distinction—who initiated him into the mysteries of Ráma worship, and taught him that anyone who pronounced Ráma's name ninety-six *crores* of times would obtain salvation. (A crore equals ten millions or one hundred lakhs.)

At the age of fourteen Tyágarája lost his father, and his mother followed her husband to the grave within a year. The cares of the household now devolved upon Tyágarája, who fulfilled his duties very conscientiously, devoutly worshipping the idols of Ráma and Sita, left to him by his grandfather and his father. By the time he had reached his thirty-eighth year he had uttered Ráma's name ninety-six crores of times, as stipulated by the *swámi*. After he had accomplished this feat, Ráma visited him while he was at his prayers. As soon as he was recognised, the god disappeared, but from that time forth Tyágarája was enabled to compose songs with perfect ease. Tyágarája's fame spread far and wide, and people flocked from remote districts to hear him. In consequence, the envy of his contemporaries was aroused, and they persecuted him. On one occasion, while he was engaged in taking his ceremonial bath of oil, a sage visited him and requested him to perform. Tyágarája sang for one hour and a half, and in recognition of his labours the sage presented him with a book and promised to return. He did not reappear in person, but revealed himself to Tyágarája in a dream, stating that he was Nárada, the patron of music. He added that he was satisfied with Tyágarája's virtue, and said that the title of the volume was "Swáranavam"; it was a rare and difficult work, but he expected Tyágarajá to master its contents, as there was much valuable information in it respecting the art of music which Tyágarája alone could appreciate and utilise. Tyágarája fulfilled Nárada's instructions, and derived great benefit from the ancient tome. The hope of seeing Ráma once more inspired him, and he continued to sing the god's praises. In his compositions he condemned the indifference of many Hindus towards the cult of Ráma, and each night, before retiring, he prepared fruit, milk and *pán* (betel nut mixed with lime) for Ráma's refreshment. In the morning he would find part of the food consumed and would eat the remainder, as it was imbued by the god with special virtue. The songs which he performed in praise of Ráma on *Ekdasi* days (the eleventh days after the new and full moons) are still extant.*

Govinda Márár was a reputed singer of Travancore to whom Ráma appeared in a dream. The god told Govinda Márár of the marvellous Tyágarája, and Govinda Márár set out upon a pilgrimage to Thiruvaiyar, where Tyágarája resided. He travelled by bullock cart, and arrived weary and exhausted after his journey. Tyágarája, who was seated with his disciples, hesitated to perform before the importunate stranger. Ultimately a *pallavi* was sung by each person present, and Govinda Márar rendered it in *shatkála* (sextuple time). He excelled in reducing the note values of his songs, and after commencing his theme in semibreves, or their equivalent, he would diminish six times over, until he concluded by rendering the melody in semidemisemiquavers. Tyágarája, who was amazed at the talent of his visi-

---

* In "Hindu Manners, Customs and Ceremonies," by Abbé J. A. Dubois, the following note occurs with reference to *Ekdasi* days: "The eleventh day of the moon is religiously observed, not only by Bráhmans, but by all those castes which have the right to wear the triple cord. They keep a strict fast on this day, abstain entirely from rice, do no servile work, and give themselves up wholly to devotional exercises."

Plate VIII.

The Tambúra.

The *Tambúra* shown above came from Northern India, and was valued by the owner at about thirty rupees. A gourd formed the bowl, whereas the body of the Southern *tambúra* is usually of wood. The *tambúra* has three steel strings and one brass string. They are played with the fingers and are never stopped. The four ivory beads seen in the photograph are known as *pusalu*, and as they are threaded upon the strings, they are movable and are employed to effect minor alterations in pitch. Pieces of quill or silk, known as *jirala*, are inserted between the strings and bridge to produce a buzzing effect.

(See the reference to Tyágarája's use of the tambúra *on page 54.)*

tor, composed a song in his honour, and Govinda
Márár prophesied that Tyágarája would revive music
in its noblest form. Govinda Márár then proceeded
to Pandharpur, where he died, and musicians make
pilgrimages to this spot, near the western frontier
of Hyderabad State, where his *tambúra* is preserved.*

The Rájas of Tanjore and of Mysore summoned
Tyágarája to their palaces, but he ignored their in-
vitations, devoting his career to the worship of
Ráma. Maharája Sarabhoji of Tanjore journeyed to
Tyágarája's home, and begged him to perform
before his nobles, but Tyágarája replied in song :
" Are these kings greater than my Ráma ?" He
begged Ráma to prevent foreigners from interrupt-
ing his work, but thereby aroused the anger of his
brothers, who desired to exploit his genius and to
accumulate wealth. To anger him, they threw his

---

* The *tambúra* of Govinda Márár had seven strings,
whereas the ordinary *tambúra*, used for drone accompaniments, has four strings only. (See the illustration.) It
is to be regretted that Govinda Márár's instrument
has perished recently. On one of the pillars in the Pan-
darinath Temple, Pandharpur, where it was preserved,
lines have been painted to represent the strings. Devotees
walk round the pillar and embrace it in honour of the great
musician. When the lines become faint through frequent
contact with the pilgrims' garments, they are restored with
a fresh coat of paint.

treasured idols into the river Káveri. Tyágarája entreated his gods to recover them, and prayed for the conversion of his materialistic kinsmen. After a year's supplication, the musician was rewarded for his unswerving trust in Ráma, when he learnt, in a dream, the spot in the bed of the river where the idols were buried, and experienced no difficulty in regaining possession of them. Moreover, his brothers became Ráma worshippers and persecuted him no longer. The songs in which he celebrated the return of his images are still preserved in Southern India. A number of miracles are attributed to Tyágarája. He is said to have restored a dead man to life by means of his art, and to have converted many of his hearers to Ráma worship. When he was about eighty-nine or ninety years of age, Ráma appeared to him and announced that he would require to be re-born once only, because the spirituality of his life on earth would be taken into account. Tyágarája sang incessantly in praise of Ráma, and prayed to remain for evermore with the celestials, without re-visiting the earth plane. At this period he composed "Raghunáyaká" and "Patti Viduvarádu," portions of which are cited at the end of this chapter. After nine months and twenty days, Ráma appeared, and agreed that Tyágarája should not be re-incarnated. Tyágarája had become a *Sunyasi*, that is to say he had entered the fourth or last stage of mortal existence, and had abandoned all worldly desire.* Ten days after the apparition the musician's face shone, and he resembled Brahmá, the Creator. His spirit ascended while miraculous flowers fell from the skies. The obsequies were performed with great magnificence, and a *Samádhi* or *Sunyasi's* tomb was erected in his memory, near which a *tulsi* (holy basil) shrub was planted which is worshipped to this day. A large concourse of pilgrims visit Thiruvaiyar each year to do honour to the genius who selected it for his home, and whose finest work was accomplished in this small town near Tanjore,

---

* Abbé Dubois, the author of "Hindu Manners, Customs and Ceremonies," described the state of *Sunyasi (Sannyasi Nirvani)* as follows: "The most holy and sublime state to which man can possibly attain is that of *Sannyasi Nirvani*, which means 'naked penitent.' In embracing this state a man ceases to be a man; he begins to be a part of the Godhead. As soon as he has attained the highest degree of perfection in this state, he frees himself voluntarily, without any trouble or pain, from his own self, and obtains *moksha*, thus becoming incorporated for ever into the Divine Self. There is no real *Nirvani* existing in this *yuga*. Those who aspire to this state must pass through twelve successive degrees of meditation and corporal penance, each one more perfect than the last. These degrees are a kind of novitiate, and each of them has a special appellation. Having at last become a *Nirvani*, the penitent no longer belongs to this world."

whilst the belief is current that great merit is acquired by performing Tyágarája's songs.

No attempt has been made to eliminate the supernatural element, so dear to the superstitious Hindu mind, from the above biography of Tyágarája, for the full meaning of his compositions would be misunderstood were his worship of Ráma to be ignored. The idea that he derived direct inspiration from his god must appeal to all believers in the divinity of music, and recalls the oft-repeated anecdote of "Papa" Haydn, who would leave his writing table and offer up a prayer for inspiration, whenever his ideas ceased to flow during the composition of his symphonies.

The following remarks respecting Tyagarája are from the pen of Mr. C. R. Sreenivas Iyengar, the learned musical critic (mentioned on page 15). They were included by him in an article which he contributed to the "Daily Express Annual" for 1925: "The psalms of David, the 'Imitation of Christ' of Thomas à Kempis, are akin to Tyágarája's hymns. They are the last word on the theory and practice of devotion, music and self-culture. . . . . They are supremely original, fresh, deep, suggestive and heart-gripping. They reveal the wonderful evolution of the soul of a neophyte right onwards until he reaches the goal. . . . . He lived his life apart from wealth, honour, patronage, crowned heads, fame and following—a poor beggar, a bitterly persecuted man, an undaunted social reformer of the true type—a fearless speaker of truth, and a peerless teacher. His hymns are so noble, so sublime, so soul-reaching, that his followers reverently speak of them as 'Tyágopanishads,' for to them they are as sacred as Holy Writ. He lived a very long life and reincarnated himself in·many an able pupil."

In a discourse on Tyágarája delivered in 1925 before the Fourth All-India Music Conference, to which further reference will be made in Chapter V, Mr. M. S. Ramaswami Iyer, of Coimbatore, the author of an excellent life of the great master, referred to the tendency of musicians in Tyágarája's youth to blend the two divisions of recitative, namely, the *Vritha*, or simple recitative, and the *Kirtana*, or sacred dramatic narrative, to which the audience supplied the choral commentary. Arunchala Kavi's volume of *vrithas* and *kirtanas*, known as "Ráma Natakam," was published in 1772, when Tyágarája was about thirteen years old, and influenced the young musician who was destined to develop Indian lyrical music. Tyágarája wrote over eight hundred *kritis*, songs, in which he united the finest characteristics of diverse styles of narrative and religious compositions, and excelled in his development of *sangathis*, or musical phrases.* He was his own author, for it is considered essential for Indian musicians to compose their own texts, and he employed the Telugu language, the most musical of Indian vernaculars, known as "the Italian of India."

With reference to Tyágarája's treatment of the *sangathis*, Mr. Ramaswami Iyer remarked : "The first *sangathi* is a very simple melody; the next is a little elaborate; the next is still more elaborate, and so on, until the last brilliant *sangathi* presents in the compass of the same *ávard* or time-limit as the first *sangathi* the maximum of rhythmic liveliness and melodic fullness.† All the *sangathis* glide into one another so easily and so gracefully that they seem to be natural evolutions and involutions of one another. Tyágarája will ever be remembered for this striking innovation, which has doubtless enriched music to an astonishing degree." In conclusion, Mr. Ramaswami Iyer stated that Tyágarája emphasised the importance of the time-honoured *tambúra* for the purpose of the drone and not of the "now-unfortunately prevailing harmonium."

* See reference to *kirtanas* and *kritis* on page 22.
† See reference to *ávard* on page 24.

The drone, which is indispensable in all public performances of Indian music, provides an effective
background to the melody, and adds the stability
which in western compositions is furnished by harmony. A drone may be played on one or two drums,
tuned either in unison or an octave apart, whilst the
víná, the *sárangí*, the *sitár* and similar instruments
possess their own drone strings. The *tambúra*, however, is regarded as the most satisfactory drone in
strument. In shape the *tambúra* is not unlike the
víná, but it is of simpler construction, without frets,
and presents few difficulties. It is played by the
fingers on the open strings, and supplies a rich
droning accompaniment. When the *amśa*, or predominant note, defined on page 12, is distinct from
the drone, the latter serves as a basic note, and the
character of the melody depends to a large extent
upon the position of the *amśa* with relation to that
of the drone. The special instrument known as the
drone or *pongi* produces only one note, the pitch of
which can be varied by means of the four or five
holes bored in this primitive instrument. The *pongi*
is played generally in conjunction with the flute or
the *nágasara*, the most common reed instrument of
India. The *nágasara* has twelve holes, of which
seven are utilised for fingering and the remainder
for the regulation of pitch. Expert players render

every variety of grace on this instrument. The Indian bagpipe, *nosbug* or *śruti upánga*, is also popular as a drone instrument. The bag, which is made of kid, is inflated by the mouth, and there are usually two cane mouthpieces, one used for the bag, and one for the drone.

Tyágarája imparted his knowledge to his faithful disciples, but he forbade those students who were endowed with a gift for improvisation to perform his own compositions, as he dreaded the mutilation of his songs. He introduced his own name into the close of his works with such phrases as: "This is the last counsel of Tyágarája." Specimens of these musical signatures will be found in the two songs below. Both were transcribed in European notation by Mr. Chinnaswami Mudaliyar, M.A., and are included in his rare "Oriental Music in European Notation," published in 1893. For the purpose of comparison the Indian versions of these songs were performed by a Telugu singer of repute, and the present author subsequently played the melodies on the piano. A few Indian critics who were present agreed that the European version conveyed only an approximate idea of the eastern interpretation. As Mr. Mudaliyar remarked in his explanatory notes: "Indian music lies under a mask at present." At the moment, however, the transcription of Indian airs into western notation, though inadequate, is the only means of removing the mask, and enabling European musicians to form some conception of the beauties which it conceals.

Raghunáyaka. Ex. 7.

Primary *rága* Sankarābharana, one of the most popular *rágas* in Southern India. See Ex. 6 below.

Rága Hamsadhvani. In Carnatic music this secondary pentatonic *rága* is used in devotional songs and love music. F (Ma) and A (Dha) are *varja*, i.e., omitted in this *rága*. G (Pa) is the *amśá*, and E (Ga), G (Pa), and B (Ni) form its characteristic phrase. The *rága* is sung at noon, and is associated with the idea of entreaty. The time *(tála)* is *Desádi*, meaning foreign, a description employed when the section commences on the fourth unit of the bar, instead of on the first.

The words are given below both in Telugu and in an English translation.[*]

---

[*] In Telugu, as in Italian, for example, certain modifications of orthography are permissible in the texts of songs for the purpose of rendering the language as harmonious as possible.

In the spelling of the text, the author has been guided by Telugu scholars, who suggested alterations in the orthography, with a view to conveying to English readers, unacquainted with Telugu, an exact idea of the sound of the words when sung.

Pallavi. This section contains the main subject of the composition. Raghunáyaká ní[1] pádayuga[2] rájívamula[3] né[4] vidazála[5] Srí.[6]

1, Ní, your; 2, Pádayuga, feet; 3, rájívamula, lotus-like; 4, né, I; 5, vidazála, cannot leave; 6, Srí, term of respect.

Paraphrase.

"Raghunáyaka!   I cannot leave your lotus-like feet."

Anupallavi.   This section contains the second subject.

Aghájalamula[1] páratholi[2] nannadarimpa[3] nívé[4] gatigáda[5] Srí[6].

1, Aghájalamula, illusion; 2, páratholi, driving away; 3, nannadarimpa, protecting me; 4, nívé, yourself; 5, gatigáda, are the saviour; 6, Srí.

Paraphrase.

"Driving away illusion and protecting me, you are the Saviour!"

Charanam.   An amplification of the above sections.

Bhavaságaramu[1] thataléka[2] né[3] bahugáṣi[4] padi[5] ní[6] marugujérithini[7]   Avanijádhipá![8]   Srítarakshaka![9] Anandakara![10]

1, Bhavaságaramu, ocean of births and deaths; 2,

thataléka, without being able to cross; 3, né, I; 4, bahugási; 5, padi, much exhausted; 6, ní, your; 7, marugujérithini, sought protection; 8, Avanijádhipá!, Lord of Sita!; 9, Srítarakshaka!, Protector of *bhaktas;* 10, Ánandakara!, ever joyful!

Paraphrase.

"Without being able to cross the ocean of births and deaths, exhausted, I sought your protection, Lord of Sita! Ever joyful Protector!"

Ex. 6. Primary Rága.

Sankarábharana Rága. Morning.

Compare with the European major mode. The difference in the sixth should be noted.

Ex. 7. Ragunáyaka.

Mela = Primary Rága.

Sankarábharana. Music and Words by
Rága Hamsadhrani Tyágarája.

Tala Désádi. *Vivace* Met. ♪ =144.

Specimen of the musical signature of Tyágarája in the
above composition.

Tyá - ga - rá - ja - nu - ta

Raghunāyaka ! nī pādayuga - rājīvamula nē vidazäla ;
Aghajālamula bāra dōlina
nnādarimpa nīvē gatigāda? Srī
Bhava sägaramu dāta lēka nē
bahu gāsi badi nī marugu jēritini
Avanijādhipā ! Srītaraksaka !
Ānandakara ! Srī Tyāgarājanuta !

The text of "Raghunāyaka" is taken from "Tyāga-
rājasvami Kīrtanalu," edited by K. V. Srinivasa Ayyangar,
Madras, 1922, page 184, a standard work amongst Carnatic
musicians.

Patti Viduvarádu. Ex. 9.

Primary *rága* Kharaharapriyá. See Ex. 8 below.
Secondary *rága* Manjari. The time (*tála*) is *Adi*,
or common time.

The words are given below both in Telugu and in
an English translation.

Pallavi. Patti[1] viduvarádu[2] ná[3] cheyi.[4]

1, Patti, holding; 2, viduvarádu, should not leave;
3, ná, my; 4, cheyi, hand.

Paraphrase.

"When once you have taken hold of my hand you
should not leave it!"

Anupallavi. Puttina[1] nádé[2] nija[3] bhaktini[4] meda[5]
gatti[6] guttu[7] chedaraka[8] brochi[9] cheyi.[10]

1, Puttina, of birth; 2, nádé, on the day; 3, nija,
true; 4, bhaktini, devotion; 5, meda, neck; 6, gatti,
tied; 7, guttu, honour; 8, chedaraka, without being
sullied; 9, brochi, protecting; 10, cheyi, hand.

Paraphrase.

"From my birth you made me your true devotee
and protected me and my honour from harm."

Charanam. Nityánityamulanu[1] bódhinchi[2] krutyákrutyamulanu[3] thélipinchi[4] pratyékudu[5] nívani[6]
kanipinchi[7] bhrutyudaina[8] Tyágaráju[9] cheyi.[10]

1, Nityánityamulanu, permanent and imperman-
ent; 2, bódhinchi, teaching; 3, krutyákrutyamulanu,
things that should be done and those that should
not be done; 4, thélioinchi, showing; 5, pratyékudu,
you the one without attachment; 6, nívani, that you;
7, kanipinchi, showing; 8, bhrutyudaina, your devotee; 9, Tyágaráju; 10, cheyi, hand.

Paraphrase.

"Taught me about things permanent and imper-
manent and showed me those that should be done,
and those that should not ¹e done, and showed me
that you are the only one without attachment. You
should not leave your devotee's (Tyágaráju) hand!"

Ex. 8.

Primary Rága.
Kharaharapriyá Rága. Noon.

Sa Ri Ga Ma Pa Dha Ni Sa
This rága is in the Dorian mode.

Ex. 9. Patti-Viduvarádu.

Primary Rága.
Kharaharapriyá
Rága Manjari.

Music and Words
by Tyágarája.

Tála Adi.

Met. ♪ = 144.

Style of execution, Preghiera, earnestly and fervently.

Notice the *Vakra* progression (i.e., crooked progression) of
the ascending scale which is identical in both tetrachords.

Arōhana (Ascent).   Avarohana or Avarō (Descent).

Sa Ga Ri Ga Ma   Pa Ni Dha Ni Sa   Sa Ni Dha Pa   Ma Ga Ri Sa

Pallavi I   *Dolce*

II

IV

III

V

VI

The latter portion is sung also a little differently, as follows :

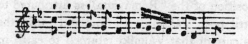

The following text of the "PATTI VIDUVARÁDU" is taken from "Tyūgarāja Ḥridayamu," edited by K. V. Srinivasa Ayyangar, Madras, 1922, Vol. II, page 359.

Patti viduvarādu nācheyi - patti viduva rādu
Puttinanādē nijabhaktini meda - gatti guttu chedaraka brōchi cheyi
Nityānityamulanu bōdhinchi - krutyā krutyamulanu thelipinchi
Pratyēkudu nīvani kanipinchi - bhrutyudaina Tyāgarāju cheyi.

Pat-ti vi-du-va-rä-du nä che-yi pat-ti vi-du-va-rä-du nä che-yi pat-ti vi-du-va-rä-du nä che-yi pat-ti vi-du-va-rä-du nä che-yi pat-ti vi-du-va-rä-du nä che-yi pat-ti vi-du-va-rä-du nä che-yi pat-ti vi-du-va-rä-du nä che-yi pat-ti vi-du-va-rä-du nä che-yi pat-ti vi-du-va-rä-du nä che-yi pat-ti vi-du-va-rä-du. Put-ti-na-nä-dē put-ti-na-nä-dē put-ti-na-nä-dē ni-ja bhak-ti-ni me-da me-da gat-ti gut-tu che-da-ra-ka brō-chi che-yi Nit-yä-nit-ya-mu-la-nu bō-dhin-chi nit-yä-nit-ya-mu-la-nu bō-dbin-chi krut-yä krut-ya-mu-la-nu the-li-pin-chi Pra-tyē-ku-du nī-va-ni ka-ni-pin-chi bhrut-yu-dai-na Tyä-ga-räju che-yi Tyä-ga-rä-ju che-yi,

The following extracts from Tyágaraja's songs, "Alakalu" and "Ennadu Zutuno," are taken also from Mr. Chinnaswami Mudaliyar's "Oriental Music in European Notation," 1893. Owing to the allusions which the songs contain to the characters in the "Rámáyana" they are of particular interest. The composition of the "Rámáyana" is attributed to the Sanskrit poet, Válmíki. In Southern India, the belief is current that Válmíki returned to earth in the person of Tyágarája, to develop the exquisite beauty of Tyágarája's *kritis** out of the recitative, associated with the "Rámáyana."

Alakalu. Ex. 10.

"Alakalu" is a song in praise of Ráma, and was inspired by the following incident in the "Rámáyana."

When Prince Ráma was sixteen years old, he was sent by his father, King Dasharatha of Ayodhya, to destroy the man-eating demons, Maricha and Suvahu, who had attacked the retreat of the sage, Vishvamitra. Ráma earned the gratitude of the hermit by killing Suvahu and wounding Maricha.

The words of the song refer to Vishvamitra's appreciation of Ráma's beauty. At the moment when

---

* See reference to Tyágarája's *kritis* on page 53.

Ráma curbed Maricha's pride, the graceful movement of the Prince's hair, stirred by the wind, enhanced Ráma's appearance. By a glance, Vishvamitra, the *rishi* of the song, indicated to Ráma the
approach of Maricha, and Ráma discharged Síva's[*]
arrow. The face of Ráma was worshipped by Tyágarája. (Ráma was endowed with half Vishnu's
divinity, and is revered throughout India as a model
son, brother and husband. He is frequently depicted
carrying a bow and arrows.)

Primary Rága, Kharaharapriyá.

Secondary Rága, Madhyamāvati. The time
(tála) is Rūpaka or triple time.

The words are given below in Telugu and in an
English translation.

Pallavi. Alakalu[1] allaladaga[2] gani[3] yaramuni[4]
yetu[5] pongeno.[6]

1, Alakalu, curved hair (of Ráma); 2, allaladaga,
moving this way and that; 3, gani, seeing; 4, yaramuni, Rája Rishi (Vishvamitra); 5, yetu, how; 6,
pongeno, pleased or rejoiced.

Anupallavi. Cheluvu[1] miraganu[2] marichuni[3]
madamu[4] anache[5] vela.[6]

---

[*] Ráma had succeeded in bending a mighty bow
which had belonged originally to the great god Síva. To
compensate Ráma, the king of Mithila had given his daugh-
ter, Sita, in marriage to the hero Ráma.

1, Cheluvu, beauty; 2, miraganu, enhanced; 3, marichuni, Maricha's; 4, ma'damu, pride; 5, anache, curbing or putting down; 6, vela, time.

Charanam. Muni[1] kanu[2] saiga[3] delisi[4] . Sivu[5] dhanuvunu[6] viriche[7] samayamuna[8] Tyágarája[9] vinutuni[10] momuna[11] ramjillu.[12]

1, Muni, Rishi; 2, kanu, eye; 3, saiga, symbol; 4 delisi, knowing; 5, Sivu, Síva's; 6, dhanuvunu, arrows; 7, viriche, breaking; 8, samayamuna, at the time of; 9, Tyágarája, Tyágarája; 10, vinutuni, admired or worshipped by; 11, momuna, in the face; 12, ramjillu, bright (hair).

Ex. 10. Alakolu.

Kharaharapriyá.   Rága Madhyamávati.*
Primary Rága.   Associated with Noon and Peace.

Sa Ri Ga Ma Pa Dha Ni Sa   Sa Ri Ma Pa Ni Si

(See Example 8, page 63).

Music and words by Tyágarája.
Tála Rúpaka. Style of execution.

Energico, Allegro con brio.   Met. ♪ = 176.
Aróhana (Ascent). Avarohana or Avaró (Descent).

Sa Ri Ma Pa Ni Sa   Sa Ni Pa Ma Ri Sa

* When the raga Madhyamávati is sung at the close of a musical entertainment, it is supposed to cancel the evil effects produced by the performance of other rágas during prohibited, or inauspicious hours. E and A are *varja* (omitted) in this rága.

Specimen of the musical signature of Tyégarája introduced into the above example of his work.

Ty - á - ga-rá - - ja

Ennadu Zutuno. Ex. 11.

"Ennadu Zutuno" is in praise of Ráma, and reference is made in it to various personages who figure in the "Rámáyana," the epic chronicle of the Solar race of Ayodhya, or Oudh. The epic records that Sita went into exile with her husband, Ráma, who was accompanied also by his brother, Laxman. Incidentally the name of Prince Laxman is associated constantly with that of Ráma in local traditions. Bharata and Chatrugna were other brothers of Prince Ráma. King Sugriva, the chief of the monkey army, assisted Ráma to regain possession of

Sita after her capture by Ravana, the demon king of Lanka or Ceylon.* Ráma's ally, Hanuman, the monkey god, is worshipped to this day as the model of a faithful servitor.

Primary Rága, Chakravaka.

Secondary Rága, Kalavati. The time *(tála)* is Madhyádi, four quavers to the bar.

The words are given below in Telugu and in an English translation.

Pallavi. Ennadu[1] zutuno[2] inakula[3] tilaka.[4]

1, Ennadu, when; 2, zutuno, will I see; 3 and 4, inakula tilaka, the *tilaka*, or caste mark on the forehead, of the Solar dynasty.

Anupallavi. Pannagasayana[1] bhakta janavana[2] punnama chanduru[3] bolu mugamunu.[4]

1, Pannagasayana, Thou resting on *adisesha*, the five-headed serpent forming Ráma's bed; 2, bhakta janavana, Thou protector of devotees; 3, punnama chanduru; 4, bolu mugamunu, Thou with a face like the full moon. (An Oriental simile indicating great personal beauty.)

Charanam. Dharanija[1] Sumitra[2] Bharata[3] Chatrugna[4] Vanarayudhapati[5] Varanjanayadu[6] karunanu[7] karikokaru[8] varnimpan[9] atharananu[10] pilchinannu[11] Tyágarájarchita.[12]

1, Dharanija, born of the earth (Sita); 2, Sumitra, son of Sumitra (Laxman); 3, Bharata, one of Ráma's brothers; 4, Chatrugna, another of Ráma's brothers; 5, Vanarayudhapati (Sugriva, the chief of the monkey army); 6, Varanjanayadu, noble Anjanaya (Hanuman, the monkey god); 7, karunanu, with love and affection; 8, karikokaru, together; 9, varnimpan, praise; 10, atharananu, with devotion, 11, pilchinannu, calling you; 12, Tyágarájarchita, Ráma worshipped by Tyágarája.

In the song Tyágarája invokes Ráma, the *tilaka* or caste mark of the Solar dynasty, who is praised and worshipped by all the personages mentioned in the text.

Ex. 11. Ennada Zutuno.

Chakravāka.   Rága Kalávati.*
Primary Rága.   Music and words by
Associated with love.   Any time.   Tyágarája.

Sa Ri Ga Ma Pa Dha Ni Sa

Tála Madhyādi.   Style of execution, with Longing and
Earnestness.
                                            M. ♩ = 144.
Arōhana (Ascent).   Avarohana or Avarō (Descent.

Sa Ri Ma Pa Dha Sa   Sa Dha Pa Ma Ga Sa Ri Sa

* B is *varja* (ómitted) in this rága and E is *varja* in the ascending scale. D is omitted in the descending scale and employed only in the ascending scale.

Specimen of the musical signature of Tyágarája introduced into the above example of his work.

Tyá - ga-rá - - ja

CHAPTER V.

THE ALL-INDIA MUSIC CONFERENCES.

SINCE the publication of Mr. Chinnaswami Mudaliyar's "Oriental Music in European Notation," various other collections of Europeanised Indian music have appeared. At the moment, Mr. G. D. Eleazar, of Madras, is engaged upon the compilation of a volume of Indian lyrics transcribed in western notation. In a recent letter to the author he enumerated some of the many difficulties he had encountered: "The difficulties one naturally finds are as follows: 1, the key signature of each *rágini*; 2, what key should be taken, i.e., what should be the tonic for a song, as all the songs cannot be written in the same key or tonic; 3, how to avoid too many sharps or flats in a *rágini*; 4, to fix the key so that it may not go beyond the compass of the human voice; 5, proper signs and abbreviations to indicate the desired effect."

All schemes of Indian notation are modern, and

formerly every air was taught by ear alone. "Not only has the Eastern no written language of a sufficiently intelligible type for his music, but he is barely able to understand, much less to master, the endless subtleties and intricacies of the celestial art as cultivated by his ancestors; he is overwhelmed by his strenuous endeavours to retain in his memory, and hand down to posterity the unwritten melodies of his great masters, most of which he has learnt solely by ear and in a mutilated form." The above extract from the preface to Mr. Mudaliyar's monumental work applies to Indian musicians of to-day as it did to those of a quarter of a century ago, but a modern campaign has been started for the uplift of Indian music from the state of degeneracy into which it has sunk.

The first All-India Music Conference, convened in 1916 by H.H. the Maharaja Gaekwar of Baroda, inaugurated several projects of reform, as will be seen by the following memorandum:

The aims and objects of the All-India Music Conference, as settled at Baroda in 1916 are as follows:

1. To take steps to protect and uplift our Indian music on national lines.

2. To reduce the same to a regular system such as would be easily taught to and learnt by our educated country men and women.

3. To provide a fairly workable uniform system of *rágas* and *tálas* (with special reference to the northern system of music).

4. To effect if possible such a happy fusion of the northern and southern systems of music as would enrich both.

5. To provide a uniform system of notation for the whole country.

6. To arrange new *rága* productions on scientific and systematic lines.

7. To consider and take further steps towards the improvement of our musical instruments, under the light of our knowledge of modern science, all the while taking care to preserve our nationality.

8. To take steps to correct and preserve permanently the great masterpieces of this sublime art now in the possession of our first-class artists and others.

9. To collect in a great central library all available literature (ancient and modern) on the subject of Indian music, and, if necessary, to publish it and render it available to our students of music.

10. To examine and fix the microtones of *śrutis* of Indian music with the help of our scientific instruments, and the first-class recognised artists of the day, and to make an attempt if possible to distribute them among the *rágas*.

11. To start an "Indian Men of Music" series.

12. To conduct a monthly journal of music on up-to-date lines.

13. To raise a permanent fund for carrying on the above-mentioned objects.

14. To establish a National Academy of Music in a central place where first-class instruction in music could be given on most up-to-date lines by eminent scholars and artists in music.

Up to the end of 1925 four conferences had taken place.* Widespread interest in music is being aroused amongst the intelligentsia of India, and it is to be hoped that the renaissance of Indian music will soon be a *fait accompli*. The second conference was held at Delhi in 1918, under the presidentship of H.H. the Nawab of Rampur, a skilled musician, and pupil of the famous Wazir Khan.† This prince furthered the cause of Indian music, by a munificent donation of fifty thousand rupees towards the establishment of a national academy of music, and allowed phonographic records to be taken of the compositions, belonging to the Tán Sen period, which are preserved in his State archives. Tán Sen, born at Gwalior, was a distinguished composer who

---

* In December, 1927, an All-India Music Conference was held in Madras.

† Wazir Khan is a lineal descendant of Tán Sen.

Plate IX.

TOMB AT GWALIOR OF THE SIXTEENTH-CENTURY MUSICIAN, TÁN SEN.

Every professional musician who visits Gwalior makes a pilgrimage to Tán Sen's grave. Near his tomb there is a tamarind tree, the leaves of which musicians and dancing girls chew, in the belief that by so doing their voices will gain in sweetness.

(See the reference to Tán Sen on pages 80 *and* 81 *and to his tomb on page* XXI.)

Plate X.

Manshar Barve with his Jalatarang or Jaltarang.

(See the description of the jaltarang on page 52 and the reference to Manshar Barve's jaltarang on page 147.)

was summoned to the Mughal court by the Emperor
Akbar (1556-1605), and homage is still paid to the
musician's tomb which is situated in his native state.*
He was renowned for his performance on the *rabáb*
or *rebáb*, a fine Muhammadan instrument. The
modern *rabáb* is furnished with four or six strings,
and is played with a horsehair bow. It is seldom
heard, but one of the few expert players of the present day is attached to the Rampur court. The late
Nawab of Rampur invented the *súr śringára*, a modern adaptation of the *rabáb*, which is played in the
same manner as the original instrument. An instrument known as the *rebeca* is still in vogue both in
Portuguese India and in Portugal; it is related to
the mediæval *rebeck*, which was introduced into
Europe by the Muhammadans, and bears marked
similarity to the *rabáb*. The descendants of Tán
Sen were assisted by the rulers of Rampur State,
many of whom have been famous patrons of music.

Besides the President, other Indian princes inter-
ested in the second All-India Music Conference were
H.H. the Maharája Holkar of Indore, H.H. the
Maharája of Nabha, and H.H. the Maharája of
Alwar.

---

* It is said that the Great Mughal gave a *crore* of rupees
to Tán Sen as a token of appreciation.

The programme of the second Conference included some fine interpretations of *dhurpad*—the pure form of Hindu song free from Muhammadan influence, introduced about 1470 by Raja Man Singh of Gwalior. *Dhurpad** is taken in slow *tempo*, and in its simple form it is devoid of any ornamentation beyond the *múrchanas†* or graces which embellish the predominant notes of the *rága*. Efficient interpreters of *dhurpad* possess voices of extensive compass, and some of the most noted of these rare artists attended the Conference, to demonstrate the particular class of work in which they specialise. After listening to their renderings one critic wrote: "The *dhurpad* style of music is becoming a rare acquisition; may God bless these living exponents of the art with long life, for there is no doubt that when these renowned artists pass away, they will leave a void in Indian art which it will be impossible to fill."

One of the curious instruments of ancient origin heard at this Conference was the *jaltarang,‡* played by Saadatkhan, of Gwalior. It consists of a number of cups containing various quantities of water.

---

* See reference to *dhurpad* on page 22.
† See reference to *múrchana* on page 21.
‡ See reference to the *jaltarang* on page 147.

The musician moistens his fingers and rubs them round the bowls, from which he can produce as many as eighteen different notes in two octaves, and Saadatkhan proved that artistic results may be obtained from this simple device. Similar cup-harmonicons figure occasionally in European music-halls, but the performers are not exclusively Oriental. A bona-fide Indian artist, however, gave an effective demonstration on the *jaltarang* in the Steinway Hall, London, about 1920, and impressed the audience by the pleasant tone which he obtained.

Professor Krishna Rao, B.A., of Mysore, read an illuminative paper before the Conference on "Emotion in Music," in which he gave a resumé of the views, explained at length, in his knowledgeable volume, "The Psychology of Music," published in 1923, in an enlarged edition, at the Guruvilas Press, Bangalore. This work contains many interesting comparisons between the music of East and West, and is worthy the attention of all students.

An arresting feature of the third All-India Music Conference, held in Benares in 1919, under the presidentship of H.H. the Maharája of Benares, was the appearance of the Baroda Indian Orchestra. The conductor was Mr. Fredilis, Principal of the Baroda School of Indian Music, and the instrumentalists included flautists and performers on the *sitár* and the

surbahár, a species of large *sitár*, which is well
adapted to the graces of Indian compositions. To
a large proportion of the audience an Indian orchestra was an innovation, and the artistic results of the
concerted music earned general approval. During
the Conference the *naubat* played every day in the
chamber above the gateway leading to the lecture
hall. The *naubat*, implying a combination of nine
instruments, is supposed to have been invented by
Alexander the Great. Formerly musicians belonging
to the *naubat* band performed at regular intervals
of three hours each, and their music was regarded
as an encouragement to the troops during periods
of warfare. The *naqqárah*, or large kettle-drum, is
included in the *naubat* band, and a special apart-
ment, known as "the *naubat* or *naqqárah khána*," is
usually reserved for musicians, above the gateways
leading to palaces and shrines. These chambers are
constructed generally with open archways on each
side through which the sound is diffused.

Lucknow, formerly a prominent centre of music
and dancing, was selected as the site of the Fourth
All-India Conference, held in January, 1925. His
Excellency, Sir William Sinclair Marris, Governor of
the United Provinces, consented to act as president,
in the absence of H.H. the Nawab of Rampur, who
was prevented from attending owing to a bereave-

ment. In his address of welcome, the Chairman of
the Reception Committee stated that a resolution in
favour of the introduction of Indian music into
schools was moved in the Legislative Council in
1924. Consequently music has become an optional
subject in the students' curriculum, and an increased
demand has arisen for trained professors.

The question of teaching Indian music on modern
lines presents serious problems. Formerly all instruction was oral; the pupil became a disciple of
his *guru* or *ustád* (teacher), who jealously guarded
the secrets of his knowledge, and revealed them only
to a few privileged followers. Diffusion of musical
learning was against the interest of the *ustáds*, who
enveloped their art in a veil of mystery, but the time
has now passed for music to be confined to one particular class of society, and authorities are beginning
to recognise the necessity for adopting a standardised method of notation as a medium of instruction.
Several interesting papers at the Conference revealed
to the audience the great diversity of opinion which
exists respecting the vexed question of notation.

At this Conference the *jaltarang* was associated
with three *sitárs*, two *dilrubas* (a variety of small
sitár), two violins, one *sárangi*, one triangle, and one
violoncello, and on this occasion the *jaltarang* was
composed of metal cylinders in place of china cups.

The youthful performer upon this musical curiosity was awarded a gold medal for his valuable participation in the items contributed by the Maihar State Band, under the conductorship of Ala-ud-din Khan.

One of the instruments most commonly heard in the Deccan is the *puñji* or *jinjivi* or *tombi*. The body and mouthpiece are made from a gourd in which two cane pipes are inserted. One of these pipes serves as the tonic drone, whilst the other is pierced with finger-holes and produces a variety of notes. It is played in *rága Nágaraválí*, a name associated with snakes, and the music produced appears to exercise a remarkable charm over serpents. The visit of the snake-charmer is of everyday occurrence, and both Europeans and Indians have recourse to his services, for the reptiles respond to the sound of his pipes with extraordinary rapidity. They creep from their holes as the musician commences his tune, and allow him to seize them and place them in his basket. Performing cobras are in great demand at Indian functions, and on these occasions they are allowed out of their baskets, and are controlled solely by the music of the *puñji*. When the melody ceases they wriggle back into captivity as though exhausted.

As a result of the All-India Music Conferences, academies and colleges are being established in various parts of the Indian Empire, and schemes are afloat for the creation of musical faculties at Indian universities. In 1919 an All-India Music Academy was inaugurated for the collection of classical music, the systematisation of *rágas* and melodies, the foundation of a central musical library, etc. In Rajputana several princes are making serious attempts to raise the standard of music at their courts, and in Southern India institutions have been started at Mysore, Tanjore, Trivandrum, and elsewhere, for promoting the study of Indian music.*

In a recent contribution to "The Times of India," Mr. Jamsheed Sohrab alluded to the unattractive demeanour of many Indian musicians as follows: "I have seen some performers who seemed to make up for lack of musical ability by facial contortions, and the most incomprehensible movements with their hands. It is most disgusting. We know that all successful orators practise gestures. I believe in this necessity, but I think that quiet, dignified ges-

---

* The following announcement appeared in "The Times of India," dated July 19, 1927. "Jamnagar, July 14. Under orders from His Highness the Maharaja Jamsaheb Bahadur, Dr. M. Fredites, Sangitacharya, Sangitamarmajna, of Baroda, has opened a college for the study of Indian music. In this college, with the aid of a staff of expert musicians, he intends to dispel the current notions about Indian music. Instruction in purely Indian music and musical instruments will be imparted in this institution."

tures should be used, and not such as are exhibited by the wandering minstrel of India." Up-to-date instructors should realise the importance of voice production, and should endeavour to dispel the idea, prevalent amongst conservative musicians, that practice ruins the voice. The antics described by Mr. Sohrab are due to the performers' lack of technique and the listeners' indifference as to the singers' deportment, for the majority of Indian audiences tolerate grimaces and harsh tones that are unbearable to Europeans.

Interest in music was awakened recently in Gujerat, and a musical conference was held in November, 1926, at Ahmedabad, under the auspices of the Gandharva Mahavidyalaya, of Bombay, one of the leading academies of Indian music. It was a sign of the emancipation of women that an Indian lady, Mrs. Vidyagauri Ramanbhai, should have been elected president. She performed her offices most efficiently and dwelt upon the importance of music as an educational factor. Pandit Vishnu Digambar, Principal of the Bombay Music School, mentioned that music had been cultivated in Gujerat in past ages, and expressed the hope that before very long every Indian child would learn music. Several concerts and competitions took place in connection with the conference.

Plate XI.

MANAHAR BARVE WITH HIS DILRUBA.

(See the reference to the dilruba on page 85 and to Manahar Barve's dilruba on page 144.)

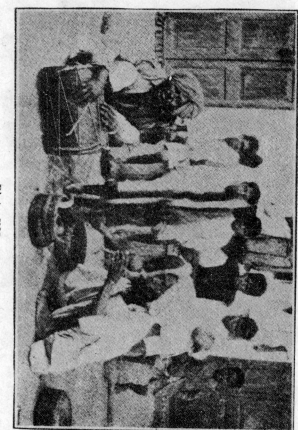

Plate XII.

A DECCAN SNAKE-CHARMER
playing on his *punji* to a cobra.

(See the description of the punji on page 86.)

CHAPTER VI.

THE ALLIANCE OF INDIAN MUSIC WITH POETRY AND DANCING.

THE words of the Tamil death songs cited below are of interest because of their musical associations. Their composition is attributed to the famous poet, Pughalénthi Pulavar, who is said to have written them during his imprisonment at the court of Chola, an ancient kingdom of the Dravidians, or aboriginal races of Southern India, and to have taught them to peasant women as they passed his windows on their way to the village well. Hindu women in general are expected to know one or more of these dirges and to sing them over the dead bodies of their near relatives. The translations of the poems are included in " Ethnographic Notes in Southern India," by E. Thurston, Madras, 1906. The plaintive music emphasises the words, which are divided into four sections :

1. THE CRY

My protector, my lord. Oh ! God.
The apple of mine eye. We cannot find
My husband, my lord. Oh ! God.
My wealth we cannot see.
Me, in my fifth year, my lord,
Me, when I was an infant.
In my tenth year, my lord,
In my milk-sucking age.
Thou, beautiful-visaged, garlanded me,* my lord,
And kept me splendidly. Etc.

3. BREAST BEATING

Oh ! protector, Oh ! my lord. Hast
Thou reached Kylas ?† Oh ! the superior, my lord,
Hast thou reached the lord of heaven? Leaving me alone.
Is it just for thee
To run away, making me solitary?
Is it right to jump away? Not separating
Even for a day, thou hast separated thyself from thy wife.
For many years not separating, why hast thou separated
    thyself? Etc.

3. HAIR SEPARATION.‡

I have untied the false hair. Oh ! my golden brother-in-law.
I have cast down the flower (from my head) on this earth.
I have loosened the string of the hair-knot, Oh ! my golden
    brother-in-law.

---

  * The reference is to the custom of exchanging garlands at marriage celebrations.

  † Kylas or Kailas. The abode of Síva, whither the blessed go after death.

  ‡ False hair, worn by married women, is exposed for sale in the bazaars in the Deccan and Southern India.

In thy side-room I have pulled off the flower,
The hair-knot that I had combed and worn. Oh! my golden
   brother-in-law.
Thou hast wrecked my usual toilet. Etc.

4. STANDING BEMOANING.

Oh! my golden brother-in-law;* Oh! my lord,
Hast thou reached the golden abode?
Me, thy most precious servant while here, Oh! my golden
   brother-in-law,
Why hast thou gone to Kylas?
Me, thy most beloved servant while here, Oh! my lord,
Why hast thou gone to the golden abode? Etc.

Words and music are very closely united in the
work of Rabindranath Tagore, and music occupies a
foremost place in the curriculum of his school at
Niketan—situated about two miles from Bolpur sta-
tion, near the home of the twelfth century musician,
Jayadeva.† Tagore frequently creates the music
before the words, and the poems are born of the
melodies which he conceives.

Delightful interpretations of poetry and music are
given occasionally in Madras, by the gifted young
poet, Harindranath Chattopadhyaya and his gifted
wife, both of whom are familiar with European
stagecraft. Mr. Chattopadhyaya's lyric powers have
earned the praise of such noted critics as Laurence

---

* "Golden brother-in-law." A term by which Tamil
women address their husbands.

† See reference to Jayadeva on pages 4, 5, 107.

Binyon, Arthur Symons and James H. Cousins. The
last-mentioned author wrote: "This young Indian
poet with some of the Shelleyan stretch of imagination and lyrical rapture, shows the way . . . . out
of the deep valleys of gloom and uncertainty into
the sunlight and elevation of inner realisation of
divinity." Harindranath Chattopadhyaya is the
possessor of an exquisitely modulated singing voice,
rich in tone and expression. He learnt voice production in Germany, and his singing to his own accompaniment is a revelation of the beauty of Indian
music at its best, and proves the truth of Captain
Day's statement that: "There *are* singers in India
whose voices are wonderfully sweet, and when they
sing their own songs in their simple form, no hearer
can doubt that, like other national music, that of
India possesses a charm peculiarly its own."

When differentiating between the music of Asia
and that of Europe, a discerning Indian critic emphasised the great contrast which exists between the
methods of constructing musical instruments in the
East from those employed in the West. A European concert artist pays much attention to the condition of the instrument upon which he is to perform, whereas the Indian musician is content to play
both solos and accompaniments on a damaged instrument. Thakur Muhammad Nawab Ali Khan,

chairman of the Reception Committee of the Conference held at Lucknow (1925), advocated reforms in instrument-making in general, and suggested, in particular, that the tone of the *vina* should be improved.*

The European violin is acquiring popularity rapidly in Southern India, and its range and power render it a formidable rival to Oriental instruments. Many Indians hold it after the fashion of a 'cello, placing the violin on the floor or divan upon which they sit, so that the instrument rests against their knees.

Some of the most primitive musical instruments have proceeded southwards into India from Tibet, and recently, interesting specimens of Tibetan wind and percussion instruments were brought into Hyderabad State. Amongst the most characteristic was a finely chased bronze bell, in shape not unlike the bell wielded by the old-fashioned English muffin-man. It had belonged to one of the chief *lamas*, and had been removed, surreptitiously, from a Buddhist temple. Tibetan death cymbals, consisting of circular pieces of metal suspended at both ends of a long cord, produce a curiously strident and resonant note, and are clashed repeatedly at funerals. Probably, the weirdest instrument of the collection, how-

---

* Detailed information respecting the work of the All-India Music Conferences is given in Chapter V.

ever, was a horn made from the bone of a goat or sheep. Holes had been pierced in the side of the instrument, and the Dravidian servants of Hyderabad soon learned to play this pipe with great zest. The value of Tibetan musical instruments is enhanced by the difficulty experienced by foreigners in procuring them, as the Tibetan authorities endeavour to prevent any curios leaving their country.

Since the broadcasting of the song of the nightingales to a 'cello accompaniment in England, in 1925, the following remarks of Sir William Jones in his treatise "On the Musical Modes of the Hindus," written in 1784, assume fresh interest.* Sir William Jones mentioned: "An intelligent Persian, who repeated his story again and again, and permitted me to write it down from his lips, declared he had more than once been present, when a celebrated lutanist, Mirza Muhammad, surnamed Bulbul, was playing to a large company in a grove near Shiraz, where he distinctly saw the nightingales trying to vie with the musician, sometimes warbling on the trees, sometimes fluttering from branch to branch, as if they wished to approach the instrument, whence

---

* A reprint of the article appeared in "Hindu Music from Various Authors," compiled by Raja Comm. Sourindro Mohun Tagore, Calcutta, 1882. See page 157 of the present volume.

the melody proceeded, and at length dropping on the ground in a kind of ecstasy, from which they were soon raised, he assured me, by a change of mode."

A link between Indian and European music is to be found in the songs of the gipsies. Magyar melodies, with their microtonic intonation, and their peculiar rhythmic stress, resemble Hindu airs, and the similarity between the gipsy music of India and of Central Europe is very marked. It is not easy to get an opportunity of hearing gipsy music in India, owing to the filthy habits and conditions of the wandering tribe. Late one evening, however, the author had the good fortune to overhear a group of gipsies singing in their camp, outside the walls of an old Rajput city. The seductive lilt of the melody, coupled with the elaborate ornamentation, reminded her of gipsy bands in Hungary. Unfortunately when she returned next day, accompanied by an interpreter to assist her in her investigations, she was informed that the band had shifted camp during the previous night. In a recent article in "The Indian Daily Mail Annual," entitled "The Gipsies—Their Indian Origin," Mr. Balak Ram, I.C.S., wrote: "It is, however, now well established that they (the gipsies) are an Indian tribe which left India at an unknown date. . . . They carried their language with them, and spoke it amongst themselves, though they learnt the speech of the country where they happened to be living for the time being. In the course of centuries the gipsies in the different countries of Europe developed separate dialects, but the basis of the dialects is one single language, which is very like what may broadly be termed 'Hindustani.' In fact, it is this feature of theirs that has enabled scholars to classify them as an Indian tribe. There is no doubt as to the correctness of the conclusions, which, however, are hardly known outside the very limited circle of students of gipsy lore."

The story of the gipsy, Valli, who was chosen by the god, Skanda, to be his second wife, is acted and sung throughout Southern India. Tamil folk-songs respecting the origins of the tribe are included in these performances, as various branches of the race have adopted Tamil as their second language, while retaining their own peculiar dialect for use amongst themselves.

The art of dancing has been closely allied to that of music from the earliest times in India. When Bráhma, the Creator, and the first person in the Hindu triad, added six *ráginis* to the principal musical *rágas*, Rambha, the celestial female, was taught the art of dancing, and imparted her knowledge to mankind Some Sanskrit authorities state that

Plate XIII.

TIBETAN INSTRUMENTS.

The Tibetan instruments shown above are: a hand-bell or *drilbu*, used in connection with religious ceremonies, death cymbals; a wind instrument made from the bone of an animal; a bell worn by all animals on the Tibetan trade route, which is reproduced as an object of interest, although it cannot be classified as a musical instrument. Miss A. L. Hardie, M.B.E., M.A., very kindly permitted the author to take this photograph for purposes of reproduction.

(See the description of these instruments on pages 93, 94 and XXV.)

Plate XIV.

INDIAN BOY DANCER DRESSED AS A GIRL.

He came from the neighbourhood of Bezwada, beyond
the Eastern frontier of the dominions of H.E.H. the
Nizam of Hyderabad.

(See the description of the dancer on pages 99 and 100.)

Bráhma taught the art of dancing to the sage Bharata, who, in his turn, imparted his knowledge to other *rishis*, and, in this manner, dancing was handed down to human beings. The heaven of Indra, on Mount Meru, was supposed to be filled with dancers and musicians. The young Srí Krishna was a gifted dancer as well as a flautist, and as he performed the *Rása* dance, "a divine dance in which divine beings took part," according to Mr. M. B. Kolatar in "Dancing in India" ("The Theosophist," April, 1918), the gods and celestial musicians rained down flowers upon him. Mr. E. B. Eastwick wrote of the dance of Srí Krishna as follows : "Such was the beautiful dance, it restored divinity to the dance of the times. Since that time, literature and the arts became full of the music of love. Manly music and dancing gave way before this subtle influence of the more tender, and more gentle, feelings of devotion and of love. Gradually the art passed into the hands of the voluptuous, who made it effeminate."*

---

* In the mystic dance, the Rás-mandala, yet imitated on the annual festival sacred to the sun-god, Heri (Heri means Krishna, familiarly called Kaniya), he is represented with a radiant crown in a dancing attitude, playing on the flute to the nymphs encircling him, each holding a musical instrument." From "Annals and Antiquities of Rajast'-han," by Colonel James Tod, London, 1829. See references to Krishna on pages 26, 105, 129, 143, xxvi, also xxvii.

Vincent A. Smith, in "The Oxford History of India," mentioned that the amusements of the Vedic period included both music and dancing. The accompaniments to the ancient dances appear to have been furnished by flute, lute and drum players. Indian dancing is a great science which has developed into a magnificent art. The "Nátya Sástra," of Bharata* included much information with respect to dancing. *Nartana*, dancing and acting, form one branch of the science of music, *Sangíta*, the other divisions being classified as *Gíta*, vocalisation, and *Vádya*, instrumentation. Dancing is subdivided into *nritta*, *vatya* and *nittrya*. *Nritta* comprises only the art of rhythmical movements, *vatya* deals with dramatic action, whilst *nittrya* is associated with nautch dancing. The ordinary musical accompaniment of the nautch is supplied by two *sárangís*, or two English fiddles, tuned in the Indian manner, one *mrdanga* or *tabla*, one *nosbug* or *śruti upánga*, and a *jalra*, or pair of cymbals.† In Indian dancing, as in Indian music, time, *tála*, may be slow, moderate or quick, *Vilamba*, *Madhya* and *Drita*.‡ The present

---

* See reference to "Nátya Sástra" on page 3.

† Descriptions of the *mrdanga*, *tabla* and *sárángi* are given on pages 28, 29, 30, and the *nosbug* or *śruti upánga* is described on page 56.

‡ See reference to *Vilamba*, *Madhya* and *Drita* on page 24.

writer has experienced considerable difficulty, however, in viewing anything but slow Indian dances. Frequently the nautch is a disappointment to European spectators, on account of the monotonous and lethargic movements of the dancers and the sameness of the musical accompaniment.

Refreshing variety to the average nautch was provided recently by a dancer-vocalist, who performed in the writer's compound, for the entertainment of Indian guests. The youth was about fifteen years old, and possessed a most intelligent and expressive face. He had been trained in his profession by experts, and his rapidity of movement and clearly defined vocalisation differed vastly from the ordinary performance of slow-footed and heavy-voiced artists. When representing the joyousness of a child, he circled round the stage with a series of light, bounding movements, curiously suggestive of certain figures in the Russian ballet, and to music of the same rhythmic character. Other steps, again, were reminiscent of clog-dancing, although he covered a larger area than the skilful clog-dancer, while the musical background of this section was emphatic, and in keeping with the nature of the dance. He was dressed like a girl, and as he was of small, slight build, the disguise was most successful. A wig of long, flowing black hair framed his face, which had been covered thickly with powder to hide his dusky skin, and his costume included the ample skirt of the dancing girl, which reached to his ankles. Many Indians present declared that never before had they seen such grace of movement in a dancer, and prophesied that the lad would revive a lost art.

In India, rural dancing frequently surpasses professional dancing in point of interest, for the peasants reveal their temperament and racial characteristics while dancing and singing. Mr. A. J. Gray included a fine description of Afghan military dances in his book, "At the Court of the Amir" (Macmillan, 1901): "The thirty soldiers formed a ring round the musicians; the drum beat a sort of slow march, and the dancers walked slowly round, singing a chant in falsetto—one half sang a verse, the other half answered. Presently, the pipes began their shrill wailing, and the dancers moved faster, with a step something like a mazurka. Quicker and quicker grew the music, and quicker and quicker the dance: turbans and shoes were tossed off without a pause. The circle widened and lessened at regular intervals, arms were waved and hands clapped simultaneously. Still continuing the mazurka step, every dancer at each momentary pause in the music whirled round on his toes to the right, then to the left. Some were, of course, more graceful than others. One in particular I noticed—a huge man with a short black beard and long wavy hair; he was a most enthusiastic and graceful dancer."

In the Ahmednagar district, to the south-west of Nagpur, the Gondhlis sing in honour of Devi during the day, and dance the *Gondhal* at night. While dancing the men wear long coats, shell necklaces and ankle bells, and they perform the *Gondhal* regularly during the *navrata* or nine nights preceding the festival of *Dasahra.*

A very interesting musical festival was held recently, near Lahore, at which a famous musician, devoted to the worship of Vishnu and Krishna, became inspired, and danced and sang in honour of his gods. The effect of his performance upon the audience was similar to that produced by Panchpakesar Bhagvatar's recitals of the "Rámáyana."* Mr. K. V. Srinivasa Ayyangar, of Madras, a famous authority on Indian music and dancing, wrote as follows respecting the art of dancing, and his words apply also to the art of Indian music: "Indian dancing involves a profound study of the passions and emotions of the human heart, and a clear and practical exposition of the same, in the most artistic form. Its main theme, therefore, is love, which, in its highest ethical aspect, transcends mere human relations and links the soul of man with the eternal God."

---

* See reference to Panchpakesar Bhagvatar on pages 2 and xxii.

Nos. 1, 2, 3 and 4 of this Appendix form amplifications of subjects previously mentioned in this work, and Nos. 5, 6 and 7 are notes on a few modern artists, Indian and European, interested in Indian Art.

EXCERPTS FROM THE "GÍTA GOVINDA."

Plate XV.

Naubat Kháṇa over a Gateway of the Mahárája's Palace at Jhalrapatan; the capital of His Highness the Maharaja Rana Sir Bhawani Singh of Jhalawar, K.C.S.I., F.Z.S., F.R.G.S., M.R.A.S., etc. View taken from the Palace Courtyard.

(See the description of the naubat kháṇa on page 84 and the reference on page IX.)

p. 104

Plate XVI.

NAUBAT KHÁNA. ANOTHER VIEW. TAKEN FROM THE ROAD LEADING TO THE PALACE.

(See Plate XV.)

I.

Excerpts from the "Gíta Govinda."

Contributed by Sir William Jones (1799).

"ASIATIC RESEARCHES," Vol. 3 (1799) contains a translation by Sir William Jones* of portions of the "Gíta Govinda," a work mentioned at the commencement of the present Study on Indian Music. The following extracts from the translation have been selected to show the importance attributed by the poet to the charm of music. The love of Krishna and Rádhá† constitutes the subject-matter of the "Gíta Govinda," and Rádhá describes her lover as follows: "Though he take recreation in my absence, and smile on all around him, yet my soul remembers him, whose beguiling reed modulates a tune sweetened by the nectar of his quivering lip, while

---

* See reference to Sir William Jones on page 157.

† See reference to Krishna and Rádhá on pages 26, 129, 180.

his ear sparkles with gems, and his eye darts amorous glances . . . . who formerly delighted me, while he gracefully waved in the dance, and all his soul sparkled in his eye." Rádhá's companion exhorts her to seek Krishna : "Advance, fervid warrior, advance with alacrity, while the sound of thy tinkling waist-bells shall represent martial music." As Rádhá enters "the mystic bower of her only beloved," she "musically sounded the rings of her ankles and the bells of her zone," and Krishna tells her that her tinkling waist-bells "yield music almost equal to the melody of thy voice."

In his article "On the Mystical Poetry of the Persians and Hindus," also included in "Asiatic Researches," Sir William Jones commented on the symbolism of Krishna worship : "Considering God in the three characters of Creator, Regenerator and Preserver, and supposing the power of Preservation and Benevolence to have become incarnate in the person of Krishna, they (the Hindus) represent him as married to Rádhá, a word signifying atonement, pacification or satisfaction, but applied allegorically to the soul of man, or rather to the whole assemblage of created souls, between whom and the benevolent Creator they suppose that reciprocal love . . . . which our most orthodox theologians believe to have been mystically shadowed in the "Song of Solomon," while they admit, that, in a literal sense, it is an epithalamium on the marriage of the sapient king with the princess of Egypt."

At the annual festival in honour of Jayadeva,[*] the entertainment consists of the performance of Jayadeva's songs, together with the representation of the "Gíta Govinda" described by Sir William Jones as "a little pastoral drama."

---

[*] See reference to Jayadeva on pages 4, 5, 91.

THE PECULIARITIES OF MANNERS AND
CUSTOMS IN HINDUSTAN TO WHICH
ALLUSIONS ARE MADE IN THEIR SONG.

II.

The Peculiarities of Manners and Customs in Hindustan to which Allusions are made in their Song.

(Extract from Captain Augustus Willard's "Treatise on the Music of Hindustan," published in Calcutta in 1834, and reproduced in Raja. Comm. S. M. Tagore's "Hindu Music from Various Authors." Calcutta, 1882.)

IT will perhaps be desirable to expatiate a little on such parts of the prevailing manners and customs of ancient Hindustan as influence their music. The songs of a nation, as well as its poetry, go a great way towards developing its domestic practices, rites and ceremonies, as also its habits of life. Those of Hindustan are very characteristic, and it is perhaps, as is justly observed, owing to this happy union of melody and poetry, when judiciously adapted to each other, that we can reconcile ourselves to the extraordinary power music is said to have anciently possessed over the human soul, not only in Hindustan, but likewise over the occidental nations, and probably over the whole world.

The allowed insignificancy of the female sex in the idea of a Hindu, the contempt with which they are generally beheld, have very considerable effects on their poetry. A transient observation should likewise be made on the Arabians and Persians, as their music is generally understood and cultivated in this country. The Hindu *Ghuzuls* are in imitation and on the model of the Persian.

In Arabic poetry the man is invariably in love with the woman who is the object beloved. In Persia he is represented, contrary to the dictates of nature, as in love with his own sex. This is evident in all lyric poems of that country. Their pieces abound with the praises of the youthful cup-bearer, the beauty of his green beard, and the comeliness of his mien. In Hindustan the fair sex* are the first to woo, and the

---

* " We must here make an allowance for *Indian* prejudices, which always assign the active part of amorous intercourse to the female, and make the mistress seek the lover, not the lover his mistress." Note on verse 255, translation of ·' Megha Duta."

I have endeavoured to assign a reason in the next paragraph after the following, which seems to me to obviate the necessity of any allowance being made for the passage on which Mr. Wilson has given this note, or of calling it a prejudice. The original text of Calidas appears to me quite natural, consistently with the customs of his country.

man yields after much courting. In compositions of this country, therefore, love and desire, hope and despair, and in short every demonstration of the tender passion, is first felt in the female bosom, and evinced by her pathetic exclamations.

If we should trace the origin of this disparity in the poetry of these nations, it will perhaps appear that the women in Arabia are less subject to be wounded by Cupid's darts, and are similar to the lukewarm beauties of Cabul. The peculiar custom of Persia is evidently the reason that their pieces abound with themes of the cast just noticed. The poor neglected women in vain expose their charms—in vain add the assistance of art to the comeliness of their persons—in vain has nature bestowed such charms, and been so lavish in her gifts to beings whom it does not much benefit. Alas! lovely creature, adorn not thy head with those precious gems, nor thy person with rich brocades; for neither these nor thy jetty ringlets, hanging gracefully down thy back, nor the reviving perfume, which thou carriest about thee, shall have any influence on the icy heart of the beloved object of thy cares—his warmth is reserved for another, he fancies superior beauties in the yet unsprung beard of his beloved Saqee, which, if it claim any attention, it is purely that it approaches to and resembles thy softness.

In Hindustan I can see no other motive but that the men being permitted, by law and the custom of the country, a plurality of wives, the women should grow fond by neglect. Having from the total want of education no means of mental amusement, they consider the society of their husbands as their supremest felicity; and as he has to bestow a portion of his time on every individual wife, it may be fairly presumed that no one of them can be cloyed with him. From this permission of polygamy she is the more solicitous to engage and secure his affections by ardent demonstrations of fondness. A precept of Hindu law should likewise be remembered, which prohibits the women to engage in the bonds of Hymen more than once during their lives. How far this precept of flagrant injustice is relished by the females, I leave the fair sex to determine.

To comprehend the songs of this country,* and to relish their beauties, we must not figure to ourselves Hindustan in the state in which it is at present but must transport ourselves back to those earlier ages to which allusions are made by them; to those times, when these regions enjoyed not the tranquillity at present subsisting in its parts, but when they were possessed by petty chieftains, arbitrary in their re-

* See reference to love songs on page 27.

spective dominions—when no highroads existed, but communication between one village and another was maintained by narrow footpaths, and rude mountains and jungles formed the natural barrier of the different chiefs, guarded by almost impossible woods, and wild beasts—when navigation by river was as impracticable as travelling by land—when a journey even to a few leagues was rendered hazardous by robbers and marauders, who infested the despicable roads, of themselves formidable, and rendered more so by frequent interruptions from rivulets and morasses, and from ravines and *nallas*, which, during the rains, presented by their rapidity and intricacies, very powerful obstacles—when topography was almost unknown, and the advice of a stranger adventitiously met was to be cautiously embraced, as robbers lurked about the roads in various disguises to seize on their prey by force or stratagem; to the time, in short, when parting even for a journey to an adjoining village, was accompanied by mutual tears, and prayers for safe return.

A distant tour such as in these days is looked upon with indifference, was formerly contemplated and consulted on for a year or two before undertaken; and when a man who had accomplished his purpose returned home in safety, after encountering all the hardships incident to it, the wonderful recital of his adventures, the skill with which he conducted himself in the presence of princes, his valour and intrepedity in times of danger, his cunning and foresight in preventing or avoiding the toils of the evil-minded, and all these exaggerated by the vanity of the traveller, formed the theme of admiration to the village, and the subject of pride to his relatives, not soon likely to be forgot.*

It is observed by the author of "An Inquiry into the Life and Writings of Homer," page 26, "that it has not been given by the gods to one and the same country to produce rich crops and warlike men, neither indeed does it seem to be given to one and the same kingdom, to be thoroughly civilised, and afford proper subjects for poetry." It is this which renders Hindustani songs flat and unpalatable, unless we transport ourselves back to their barbarous and heroic ages. Their abhorrence of innovation induces them to retain their ancient ways of thinking, or at least to imitate their manner of thinking in times of yore, notwithstanding the changes introduced by time. Indeed, from what has been observed in this and the preceding paragraph, although

---

* For information respecting the insecurity of Indian roads until the nineteenth century, see Meadows Taylor's "The Confessions of a Thug," The World's Classics, 1901. Another edition abridged and annotated, Bombay, 1922.

to those whose hearts are not afflicted by separation, then it is that she feels her existence insupportable. Cheering hope, which beguiled her during the former seasons, no longer affords its balmy aid, and she despairs of his arrival this year. Every cloud, every flash of lightning sends forth a dart to her tender bosom, and every drop of rain adds fresh poignancy to the wound in her agonising heart. If she endeavours by domestic toils to wean her thoughts for a moment from her absent lover, the *coel*, and particularly the *pupeeha*, reminds her of him by her constant and reiterated interrogations of *Pee-cuhan, Pee-cuhan*?

These, however, are not the only birds which are addressed by the females of Hindustan by the title of *byree* or enemy; the peacock,* the *chatak*, and

---

the expected return of such persons as are at this time absent from their family and home." Note on line 20 of the translation of the "Megha Duta," by H. H. Wilson, Esq.

"Sprang from such gathering shades to happier sight."

The meaning of Calidas seems to be somewhat different.

And a hundred Hindustani songs will prove that after the rains are set in, it is no season for travelling.

* "Or can the peacock's animated hail,
    The bird with lucid eyes, to lure thee fail?"

"The wild peacock is exceedingly abundant in many parts of Hindustan, and is especially found in marshy places; the habits of this bird are in a great measure aquatic, and the setting in of the rains is the season in which they pair; the

several others are said to add to their affliction, and remind them of their absent lovers. Superstition lends her aid to afflict or comfort them, by attaching importance to the throbbing of the eyes or pulsations of the limbs.*

The husband remaining from home for several years together, his wife, if she had been married very young, when she attains the years of maturity, begins to feel the power of love, and readily finds a youth on whom she fixes her affections,† having perhaps little more knowledge of her absent husband than from hearsay. In such a state of things, the lover can seldom be admitted at home on account of the smallness of the house, and the number of relatives. She sees herself therefore reduced to the necessity

---

peacock is therefore always introduced in the description of cloudy or rainy weather, together with the *cranes* and *chatakas*."—"Cloud Messenger," pp. 1, 29, 148.

   * "O'er her left limbs shall glad pulsations play."

"Palpitation in the left limbs, and a throbbing in the left eye, are here described as auspicious omens when occurring in the females; in the male, the right side is the auspicious side, corresponding with the ideas of the *Greeks*, described by Potter, *q.v.*"—*Ibid.*

   † An objection very frequently started by Europeans against Hindu poetry and songs is, that they are generally too licentious and voluptuous. To such I would recommend the perusal of the note by Mr. Wilson on line 468 of his translation of the "Megha Duta." It is too long to quote.

of visiting him* at his, to effect which, it requires a
great deal of circumspection and evasive art. The
female sex being generally more fond affords a fer-
tile source of dread from the influence of rivals. It
is undeniable that such practices are immoral; but
such is the fact, and nature, unrestrained by education (and the women of Hindustan are perfectly ignorant of all knowledge but the art of pleasing) will
positively have its headlong course. . . . .

The tenor of Hindustani love-ditties, therefore,
generally, is one or more of the following themes :

1. Beseeching the lover to be propitious.

2. Lamentations for the absence of the object
beloved.

3. Imprecating of rivals.

4. Complaints of inability to meet the lover from
the watchfulness of the mother and sisters-in-law,
and the tinkling of little bells† worn as ornaments

---

* "The pearls that bursting zones have taught to roam,
  Speak of fond maids, and wanderers from home."

"I have already mentioned that the Hindus always send
the lady to seek her lover, and they usually add a very reasonable degree of ardour and impatience."—Note on line 466,
Wilson's "Megha Duta."

† "My fair awakens from her tinkling zone."

"A girdle of small bells . . . . is a favourite Hindu ornament; also silver circles at the ankles and wrists, which emit
a ringing noise as the wearer moves."—Wilson's "Megha
Duta," pp. 1, 85, 514.

The use of this ornament was probably first imposed by

round the waist and ankles, called *payel*, *bichooa*, etc.

5. Fretting, and making use of invectives against the mother and sisters-in-law, as being obstacles in the way of her love.

6. Exclamation to female friends termed *Sukhees*, and supplicating their assistance; and

7. *Sukhees* reminding their friends of the appointment made, and exhorting them to persevere in their love.

---

jealous husbands to check clandestine visits, should the wives be so inclined; the sound emitted by them rendering them more liable to detection; until women using them being regarded more chaste, others were obliged to comply with the fashion to avoid aspersion of character. Thus did the Hindus endeavour to fetter their wives, and secure their affections by such inadequate means; neglecting their moral instruction, which is the only safe barrier.

See reference to Rádhá's bells on page 105.

INDIAN MUSIC IN STAFF NOTATION IN RELATION TO MR. E. CLEMENTS'S WORK.

III.

Indian Music in Staff Notation in relation to Mr. E. Clements's Work.

ONE of the staunchest supporters of Indian music is Mr. E. Clements, I.C.S., author of the informative work, "Introduction to the Study of Indian Music," Longmans, 1913. In 1926, Mr. Clements was honoured by an invitation to deliver a series of lectures on music at the Bombay University, and proved to be as interesting a lecturer as he is a writer. In his introductory lecture he referred to Carnatic music, and mentioned that this branch of Indian music has probably undergone less change than any other during the past two thousand years. His remarks with reference to the septimal intervals revealed by a careful analysis of the Carnatic scale, and the intervals favoured by the Greeks in the early Christian era, suggested interesting ethnographical speculation.

In his book Mr. Clements proves himself to be a remarkably clear thinker. The sub-title of his "Introduction to the Study of Indian Music" summarises this work as: "An attempt to reconcile modern Hindustani music with ancient musical theory, and to propound an accurate and comprehensive method of treatment of the subject of Indian musical intonation," whilst in the first chapter the author states that his volume does not extend beyond the province of intonation as an introduction to the study of Indian music. Despite its limitations, his treatise is one of the most instructive studies on Hindustani music published in English during the present century, and contains many valuable comments on the subjects of equal temperament and staff notation in relation to Indian melody. All performers and publishers should heed Mr. Clements's warning on page 35: "One can only conclude that Indian writers who openly advocate the use of tempered instruments are unaware of their utter inadequacy to give any idea of Indian intonation. A word of warning appears to be needed by others, who, although not in favour of tempered music, are ensnared by Western notation. They should remember that Western notation, without drastic changes, such as those here recommended, is as detrimental to their music as the tempered harmonium. It is a tempered notation.

. . . . The keys of Western music with their key-signatures are part and parcel of the tempered system, and are not suited to the Indian *rágas*." Mr. Clements graphically explains his theories respecting the adequate transcription of Indian music into staff notation, and mentions the patient research of Mr. K. B. Deval, a retired deputy collector. In 1910 Mr. Deval published the results of his investigations into Indian intonation in " The Hindu Musical Scale and the Twenty-two Śrutees (Śrutis)," Arya Bushan Press, Poona, for which Mr. Clements wrote an introduction. The harmonium tuned in the twenty-two śrutis, to which reference is made on page 32 of the present study, was designed by Mr. H. Keatley Moore, B.A., at the instigation of Mr. Deval.

At the present time one of the greatest needs of musical India is the conservation of her national music, and the judicious employment of staff notation for this purpose may prove of value. Editors, however, should remember that the characteristics of Indian melody may be lost through the use of staff notation, unless explanations are furnished as to the difference between the Indian and European scale. India is rich in folk-song, and a vast field of useful activity is open to experts willing to collect the indigenous tunes which reveal the soul of the people, but, to quote again from Mr. Clements : " Those who

invent notations no better than others already in existence, with an elaborate superfluity of new and
wonderful signs, in the hope of handing their names
down to posterity as inventors, are friends of doubt-
ful sincerity. Those who use the staff-notation for
the purpose, without attempting to distinguish the
special features of Indian notation, are encouraging
the heresy that intonation is of minor importance."

The present writer's attention was much attracted
by peculiar folk-songs which she heard in remote
parts of Telingana in Southern India. They were
characterised by sharply-defined rhythm, which was
accentuated during the course of performance by the
clash of small cymbals and the beating of drums.
Unfortunately her attempts to record them in staff
notation proved fruitless, owing to the elusive character of the melody.

Commenting on the generality of southern folk-
song in "The Music and Musical Instruments of
Southern India and the Deccan," Captain Day
wrote: "The ordinary folk-songs of the country are
called *lavanis*, and will be familiar to everyone
who has heard the coolies sing as they do their work;
the women nursing their children; the bullock
drivers; *dhooly* bearers; or sepoys on the march.
The airs are usually very monotonous. The words, if
not impromptu, are a sort of history or ballad in

praise of some warrior or *burra Saheb*. Some have
a kind of chorus, each man in turn singing an im-
provised verse. . . . .

"At the time of the *Káma* festival in honour of the
Indian god of love, special *lavanis* called *Saval*,
are sung. The words of these are sung by two par-
ties—one called *Turai* and the other *Kalki*—intended to represent the god Krishna and his mistress Rádhá.* Questions of a metaphorical nature
are sung by one party and answered by the other.
These were formerly sung extempore, but their performance is now usually rehearsed beforehand. This
species of entertainment is also practised in Northern
India under the name of *Kabi.*"

---

* See reference to Krishna and Rádhá on pages 26, 105
and 180.

DAROOL-OOLOOME SANGIT-HIND.

IV.

Darool-ooloome Sangit-Hind.

(Academy of Indian Music).

THE well-known writer and lecturer, Atiya Begum (Begum Saheba Fyzee-Rahamin), advocates the establishment of an Academy of Indian Music at New Delhi. With its magnificent Secretariat, its sumptuous Viceregal Lodge, its imposing parliament buildings, and its many palaces belonging to ruling princes, the new capital is becoming the hub of the Indian Empire. If erected amid such surroundings a college of music would acquire immediately national importance, and Atiya Begum is untiring in her efforts to establish a central institution where a systematic training in Indian music could be obtained, and to which branch schools could be affiliated. In 1916 this gifted lady helped to initiate the first All-India Music Conference, under the distinguished patronage of His Highness the Maharaja Gaekwar of Baroda, and in great measure it is due to her efforts that a music school was opened in Lucknow at the close of 1926. In 1913, Atiya Begum's book on Indian music was published in London, and in the same year she lectured in Paris at the Sorbonne. Several artistic functions were arranged in the French capital, which assisted her propaganda work, and in 1914 she was invited to lecture in Holland, Germany and Austria. The outbreak of war interfered with her project of staging an Indian opera in Brussels, but after her return to India she decided to visit America, and in 1918-19 she lectured in most of the important cities in the U.S.A. Her second volume on the music of India was published by Luzac and Co. in 1926, and the third volume is in course of preparation. Owing to the very close relationship between Indian music and Indian dancing, the fourth volume, which is still in manuscript, deals exhaustively with Indian dancing.

THE INDIAN DANCES OF THE
DENISHAWN DANCERS.

The Indian Dances of the Denishawn Dancers.

DURING their 1925-6 tour in Asia, Miss Ruth St. Denis and Mr. Ted Shawn were much impressed by the dancing and music of India, and their "Souvenir Programme," published shortly after their return to the United States, contains a remarkable description of the cosmic dance of Síva, taken from the volume entitled "The Dance of Síva," by the great authority on Indian music, Dr. Ananda Coomaraswamy. The symbolism of Síva's dance is described as follows: "The essential significance of Síva's dance is threefold: first, it is the image of his Rhythmic Play as the Source of all Movement within the Cosmos, which is Represented by the Arch; secondly, the Purpose of his Dance is to Release the Countless souls of men from the Snare of Illusion; thirdly, the Place of the Dance, Chidambaram, the Centre of the Universe, is within the

Heart." Mr. Ted Shawn, who made a special study
of Síva as "Natarája," or "Lord of the Dance," re-
presents the Indian god in Miss St. Denis's production, "The Cosmic Dance of Síva," for which music
has been specially composed by Lily Strickland
Anderson, a gifted American composer, who has resided in India for many years, where she has learnt
to reproduce the subtle charm of Indian music.*

In British India, European tourists have few
opportunities of witnessing fine Indian dancing.
Consequently it is unwise for travellers, who have not
the good fortune to attend private performances in
the palaces of Indian princes and noblemen, to pass
criticism upon the art of the nautch in general.
Many dancing girls possess considerable dramatic
talent, and by gesture and facial expression alone
they reveal the meaning of their songs to listeners
who do not understand the words. They are genuine artists, and the instrumentalists follow every
movement and intonation of the soloists with rapt
attention, with the result that the accompaniment
becomes an integral part of the entertainment.

The peacock dance is one of the most graceful
items to be seen in the Deccan. The exponents man-

---

* In the Indian Museum, Calcutta, there is a remarkable
bronze statue of Síva Natarája which reveals the majesty
of Síva's cosmic dance.

ipulate their voluminous skirts until their draperies resemble the outstretched tail of the peacock, while the graceful movements of their arms, hands and fingers represent the fluttering of the bird. They sing tender love lyrics, in which they lament upon the absence of their lovers and describe the devotion of the peacock to its mate.

In many parts of India there are records of the sweet-voiced singers of the past, and one such interesting relic is to be found near Hyderabad City (Deccan). A few miles outside the city walls there is a large tomb, surrounded by a beautiful garden, in memory of Chandaji, a famous dancer at the court of Hyderabad during the reign of Nizam Sikandar Jah (1803-1829). Chandaji accumulated great wealth and was highly-educated. She lived at a period when the education of Indian women was confined mainly to dancing-girls, and by means of her art and her general knowledge she became an influential personality who was treated with great respect.

MANAHAR G. BARVE.

An Appreciation.

MANAHAR G. BARVE.

AN APPRECIATION.

"MASTER" MANAHAR G. BARVE, as he is styled on his posters, is an Indian musical prodigy, still in his teens, who has justly acquired fame in India, Burma and Ceylon, and proposes to visit Europe. He performs on a large number of Oriental instruments, and the present author is greatly indebted to him for his kindness in permitting the reproduction of several photographs. Moreover, Barve very graciously consented to sit for the photographer in order to illustrate the methods of playing the instruments. On the concert platform, he wears a wonderful scarf, decorated with nearly two hundred gold and jewelled medals, which have been presented to him as tokens of appreciation, and for this reason the scarf appears in his photographs.

When dressed as Srí Krishna, Barve enthralls his listeners by his remarkable performance on the flute. After attending his concerts in the Jubilee Hall,

Rangoon, one correspondent wrote: "What most attracted the people was his playing on the flute. The boy, standing as he was on the stage, in Srí Krishna's attire, represented Srí Krishna incarnate, and carried away the audience into the heavenly region by the melodious notes of his *bansri* (flute)."[*] Manahar Barve is thoroughly acquainted with the *rágas*, and, although a Maratha[†] by birth, he interprets the *kírtánas* of Tyágarája with the skill of the most accomplished Southerner. A linguist as well as a vocalist and instrumentalist, he sings in several Indian tongues, including Hindi, Urdu, Marathi, Telugu and Tamil, and, in consequence, his interpretations are not marred by inadequate translations of the texts of his songs.

Some of Barve's most attractive items consist of his solos on the *dilruba*, a string instrument which is popular in Bombay Presidency and the Deccan. It is usually about two feet in height, and is furnished with four main metal strings and a large number of sympathetic understrings.

---

[*] See reference to Krishna on pages 26, 97, 105, 129, xxvi and xxvii.

[†] Sir William Wilson Hunter, in "The Indian Empire," describes Maháráshtra as "stretching from the Berars in Central India to near the south of the Bombay Presidency." —Page 376 of third edition, London, W. H. Allen and Co., Ltd., 1393.

Plate XVII.

MANAHAR BARVE WITH HIS SÁRINDA.

(See the reference to Manahar Barre's sárinda on page 146.)

Plate XVIII.

MANAHAR BARVE WITH HIS SARASAROJ.

(See the reference to Manahar Barve's sarasaroj on page 146.)

He uses a *sárangí** about one and a half
feet in length, which appears to be a diminutive edition of the instruments employed in Rajputana, to
which reference was made in the foregoing pages.
Barve's *sárangí* is a relic of his earliest childhood,
when he was too small to perform on powerful string
or percussion instruments. At a recent concert in
Secunderabad, Deccan, he played *sárangí* solos to
the accompaniment of the harmonium, the *mrdanga*†
and the triangle. In the hands of his father,
Professor Ganpat Gopal Barve, the triangle as-
sumed the rôle of conductor's baton, and very fine
ensemble playing was the result. The most distinctive feature of this performance, apart from Manahar Barve's solo work, was the skill of the *mrdanga*
drummer, who excelled in complicated rhythmic and
syncopated effects. The *mrdanga* and the *tabla*‡
formed the background to most of the numbers on the programme, and, as the entertainment
lasted for over four hours, the drummer's office was
no sinecure. The unpleasant tones of the harmonium
were heard too frequently for perfect enjoyment during the course of the evening. The instrument em-

---

* See reference to the *sárangí* on page 30.
† See reference to the *mrdanga* on page 28.
‡ See reference to the *tabla* on pages 28 and 29

ployed, however, was of better quality than the cheap
Austrian harmoniums which are general throughout
India, and a harmonium and *mrdanga* duet, with
Manahar Barve at the former instrument, was a *tour
de force* which compelled admiration. Barve also
plays on the *sárinda*—a small string instrument employed by the beggars of Karachi and
Bengal. It has only two strings, and might be described as "a poor relation of the *sárangi.*" Barve
possesses a very fine *sitár,*[*] from which he obtains a round, full tone, and his performances
upon this instrument have aroused particular interest
in Southern India, where it is not so well known as
it is in the Deccan and further north. He is popu-
larising the *sarasaroj*, a species of dulcimer, in tone
resembling the harpsichord, which is played with
two sticks and has sixteen strings.

Amongst the many accomplishments in which
Barve excels is the peculiar skill required for increasing speed by the diminution of note values, mentioned with reference to Govinda Márar.[†] "Master"
Prabhakar, a clever little lad, known as "The Indian
Cuckoo," assists "Master" Barve, and possesses considerable technique and breath control, although his

---

[*] See reference to the *sitár* on page 37.
[†] See page 48.

voice is feeble. He sang in "Khamaj," or "Khambaz," a cheerful *rāga* associated with the idea of love, which may be performed at any hour. Barve applies the name *sundari*, meaning "beautiful," to a type of flute used at Karachi, although the same title is sometimes used with reference to the *sitár*. Barve's *sundari* is a tiny instrument, the tone of which is thin and monotonous, but it is suitable for the production of bird-like notes.

Some of the most effective percussion instruments which figure in Barve's programmes are his Burmese gongs, consisting of three rows of metal discs fixed in wooden cases. Each frame holds four discs, and the pitch is dependent upon the size of the circular pieces of metal. The box containing the largest disc is placed on the performer's left, whilst the treble or smallest gongs remain on the player's right. His *jaltarang* or *jalatarang*,* a collection of china bowls, consists of fifteen basins, the largest of which is about the size of a family pudding basin, whereas the smallest is no bigger than an afternoon tea-cup without a handle. The bowls are placed on the floor in a semi-circular wooden stand containing canvas-lined niches, each

---

* See reference to the *jaltarang* on page 82.

one of which is numbered to correspond with the numbers on the basins.

Professor Ganpat Gopal Barve has drawn up some very ingenious charts showing the connection between Eastern and Western music. By way of illustration, he has published European airs in staff notation, with indications in Gujerati as to the manner of performance, and it is perfectly feasible for an English and an Indian musician to sing the tunes in unison from the printed instructions, although neither performer can understand the signs which guide his colleague. Professor Barve has established a school of music in Bombay, where numerous experiments are made with regard to the scientific value of music. He is extremely interested in colour music, and believes in the medicinal value of the art, a conviction which is shared by many Indian and European musical authorities. At the second All-India Music Conference, held in 1918, at Delhi, Mr. Ganpatrao K. Chavan referred to the healing properties of Indian music as follows : "One of the subtle remedies which should be given more consideration is music. The idea that music may be so applied as to actually heal the diseases of the human organism, is in perfect keeping with the advanced thought of the age. The effect of harmonious sounds on the mind is recognised as beneficial, as it appears to do its good by bringing about regularity and rhythm and soothing perturbed mind. The human physical mechanism is so based as to divide and sub-divide so many nerves, which start their course like net-work from the spinal cord, which is the chief nerve centre and is connected with the brain. Music can greatly help to harmonise the discord caused in the human organism by various mental and physical ills. Of course, music should be prescribed with due regard to the nature and kind of the mental and physical condition to be treated."

The theories evolved by Professor Barve respecting the classification of melodies according to their curative properties are instructive and suggestive. When given publicity they should win speedy recognition both in Europe and Asia.

INDIAN MUSIC AND THE WORK OF
SUFI INAYAT KHAN.

Plate XIX.

MANAHAR BARVE WITH HIS SUNDARI.

(See the reference to Manahar Barve's sundari on page 146.)

p. 152

in the chair. Inayat Khan was firmly convinced of the spiritual power of music, and many seekers after truth who visited his London studio, had the opportunity of attending fine performances of Indian music and drama, while becoming acquainted with Inayat Khan's philosophy.

In Europe and in the U.S.A. Inayat Khan founded the Súfi Order of Universal Brotherhood, which embraced mysticism, religion, philosophy, literature and music. The headquarters of this movement, which is distinct from the Súfism of Islam, are situated at Geneva, and Inayat Khan established a summer school at Suresnes, near Paris, where many of his disciples and collaborators were awaiting him at the time of his death. He had been absent from India for sixteen years, and was on a short visit to his fatherland, when he was cut off in the midst of his labours. The sympathies of Inayat Khan were universal, and he appreciated European as well as Oriental music. One of the treasured possessions of the present writer is a letter of thanks addressed to her by Inayat Khan, after a recital of poetry and music, given by her in London in 1916, at the annual reception of the Súfi Order.

Indian Music and the Work of Sufi Inayat Khan.

SUFI INAYAT KHAN, who passed away in
Delhi on February 5, 1927, laboured long and
hard for the cause of Indian music, and through his
influence many Westerners learnt to appreciate its
peculiar beauty. Inayat Khan was born in Gujerat
of a musical family, and his grandfather, Moula Bux,
invented a system of notation, in addition to estab-
lishing a school of music in Baroda State. His
Highness the Gaekwar of Baroda interested himself
in the education of Inayat Khan, who showed marked
talent for music and poetry at an early age, and,
when still quite young, Inayat Khan embarked upon
a mission for the uplift of Indian music He devoted himself to artistic propaganda for some nine
years, during which period he spoke in many of the
large Indian cities, and lectured at the University
Institute, Calcutta, with Dr. Rabindranath Tagore

ON THE MUSICAL MODES OF THE HINDUS.

VIII.

On the Musical Modes of the Hindus.

Written in 1784, and since much Enlarged by the Author.*

[The following treatise on Indian Music by Sir William
Jones (1746-94) is reproduced from the third volume of "Asiatic Researches," 1799, a rare work, described on the title-
page as the "Transactions of the Society instituted in Bengal for inquiring into the History and Antiquities, the Arts,
Sciences and Literature of Asia."

Sir William Jones founded the Asiatic Society in 1784,
shortly after his arrival in Calcutta. He was a great scholar
and remarkable linguist, possessing a thorough knowledge of
thirteen languages. He was acquainted with the theory of
music, and his essay is one of the earliest and most interesting contributions by an English writer to the study of
Indian music.

A reprint of the treatise is included in "Hindu Music
from Various Authors," compiled by Raja Comm. Sourindro
Mohun Tagore, Calcutta, 1882.]

M USICK belongs, as a *Science*, to an interesting
part of natural philosophy, which by mathematical deductions from constant phenomena,

---

* Sir William Jones was president of the Asiatic Society
for many years.

explains the causes and properties of sound, limits
the number of mixed, or *harmonick*, sounds to
a certain series, which perpetually recurs, and fixes
the ratio, which they bear to each other, or to one
leading term; but, considered as an *Art*, it combines
the sounds, which philosophy distinguishes in such a
manner as to gratify our ears, or affect our imagina-
tions, or, by uniting both objects, to captivate the
fancy while it pleases the sense, and speaking, as it
were, the language of beautiful nature, to raise correspondent ideas and emotions in the mind of the
hearer; it then, and then only becomes what we call a
fine art, allied very nearly to verse, painting and
rhetorick, but subordinate in its functions to pathe-
tick poetry, and inferior in its power to genuine
eloquence.

Thus it is the province of the *philosopher*, to discover the true direction and divergence of sound pro-
pagated by the successive compressions and expan-
sions of air, as the vibrating body advances and re-
cedes; to show why sounds themselves may excite a
tremulous motion in particular bodies, as in the
known experiment of instruments tuned in unison;
to demonstrate the law, by which all the particles of
air, when it undulates with great quickness, are con-
tinually accelerated and retarded; to compare the
number of pulses in agitated air with that of the

vibrations, which cause them : to compute the veloci-
ties and intervals of those pulses in atmospheres of
different density and elasticity; to account, as well
as he can, for the affections, which musick produces;
and, generally, to investigate the many wonderful
appearances, which it exhibits : but the *artist*, without considering, and even without knowing, any of
the sublime theorems in the philosophy of sound,
may attain his end by a happy selection of *melodies*
and *accents* adapted to passionate verse, and of *times*
conformable to regular metre; and, above all, by
modulation, or the choice and variation of those
modes, as they are called, of which as they are contrived and arranged by the *Hindus*, it is my design,
and shall be my endeavour, to give you a general
notion with all the perspicuity, that the subject will
admit.

Although we must assign the first rank, trans-
cendently and beyond all comparison, to that powerful musick, which may be denominated the sister of
poetry and eloquence, yet the lower art of pleasing
the sense by a succession of agreeable sounds, not
only has merit and even charms, but may, I persuade
myself, be applied on a variety of occasions to salu-
tary purposes; whether, indeed the sensation of hearing be caused, as many suspect, by the vibrations of
an elastick ether flowing over the auditory nerves

and propelled along their solid capillaments, or whether the fibres of our nerves, which seem indefinitely divisible, have, like the strings of a lute, peculiar vibrations proportioned to their length and degree of tension, we have not sufficient evidence to decide; but we are very sure that the whole nervous system is affected in a singular manner by combinations of sound, and that melody alone will often relieve the mind, when it is oppressed by intense application to business or study. The old musician, who rather figuratively, we may suppose, than with philosophical seriousness, *declared the soul itself to be nothing but harmony*, provoked the sprightly remark of CICERO, that he *drew his philosophy from the art which he professed;* but if, without departing from his own art, he had merely described the human frame as the noblest and sweetest of musical instruments, endued with a natural disposition to resonance and sympathy, alternately affecting and affected by the soul which pervades it, his description might, perhaps, have been physically just, and certainly ought not to have been hastily ridiculed: that any medical purpose may be fully answered by musick, I dare not assert; but after food, when the operations of digestion and absorption give so much employment to the vessels, that a temporary state of mental repose must be found, especially in hot cli-

mates, essential to health, it seems reasonable to believe, that a few agreeable airs, either heard or
played, without effort, must have all the good effects
of sleep and none of its disadvantages; *putting the
soul in tune*, as MILTON says, for any subsequent
exertion; an experiment, which has often been success-
fully made by myself, and which any one, who
pleases, may easily repeat. Of what I am going to
add, I cannot give equal evidence; but hardly know
how to disbelieve the testimony of men, who had no
system of their own to support, and could have no
interest in deceiving me: first, I have been assured
by a credible eye witness, that two wild antelopes
used often to come from their woods to the place,
where a more savage beast, SIRAJUDDAULAH, entertained himself with concerts, and that they listened
to the strains with an appearance of pleasure, till the
monster, in whose soul there was no musick, shot one
of them to display his archery: secondly, a learned
native of this country told me, that he had frequently seen the most venomous and malignant
snakes leave their holes, upon hearing tunes on a
flute, which, as he supposed, gave them peculiar delight; and, thirdly, an intelligent *Persian*, who repeated his story again and again, and permitted me
to write it down from his lips, declared he had more
than once been present, when a celebrated lutanist,

12

Mírzá MUHAMMAD, surnamed BULBUL, was playing to a large company in a grove near *Shiraz*, where he distinctly saw the nightingales trying to vie with the musician, sometimes warbling on the trees, sometimes fluttering from branch to branch, as if they wished to approach the instrument, whence the melody proceeded, and at length dropping on the ground in a kind of ecstasy from which they were soon raised, he assured me, by a change of mode.

The astonishing effects ascribed to musick by the old *Greeks*, and, in our days, by the *Chinese*, *Persians*, and *Indians*, have probably been exaggerated and embellished; nor, if such effects had been really produced, could they be imputed, I think, to the mere influence of sounds, however combined or modified; it may, therefore, be suspected (not that the accounts are wholly fictitious, but) that such wonders were performed by musick in its largest sense, as it is now described by the *Hindus*, that is, by the union of *voices*, *instruments*, and *action;* for such is the complex idea conveyed by the word *Sangíta*, the simple meaning of which is no more than *symphony*; but most of the *Indian* books on this art consist accordingly of three parts, *gána*, *vádya*, *nritya*, or *song*, *percussion* and *dancing;* the first of which includes the measures of poetry, the second extends to instrumental musick of all sorts, and the third includes the whole compass of theatrical representation. Now it may easily be conceived, that such an alliance, with the potent auxiliaries of distinct articulation, graceful gesture, and well adapted scenery, must have a strong general effect, and may, from particular associations, operate so forcibly on very sensible minds, as to excite copious tears, change the colour and countenance, heat or chill the blood, make the heart palpitate with violence, or even compel the hearer to start from his seat with the look, speech, and actions of a man in a phrensy: the effect must be yet stronger, if the subject be *religious*, as that of the old *Indian* dramas, both great and small (I mean both regular plays in many acts and shorter dramatick pieces on *divine love*) seems in general to have been. In this way only can we attempt to account for the indubitable effects of the *great airs* and impassioned *recitative* in the modern *Italian* dramas, where three beautiful arts, like the Graces united in a dance, are together exhibited in a state of excellence, which the ancient world could not have surpassed and probably could not have equalled; an heroick opera of METASTASIO, set by PERGOLESI, or by some artist of his incomparable school, and represented at *Naples*, displays at once the perfection of human genius, awakens all the affections, and captivates the imagination at the same instant through all the senses.

When such aids, as a perfect theatre would afford, are not accessible, the power of musick must in proportion be less; but it will ever be very considerable, if the words of the song be fine in themselves, and not only well translated into the language of melody, with a complete union of musical and rhetorical accents, but clearly pronounced by an accomplished singer, who feels what he sings, and fully understood by a hearer, who has passions to be moved; especially if the composer has availed himself in his *translation* (for such may his composition very justly be called) of all those advantages, with which nature, ever sedulous to promote our innocent gratifications, abundantly supplies him. The first of those natural advantages is the variety of *modes*, or *manners*, in which the *seven* harmonick sounds are perceived to move in succession, as each of them takes the lead, and consequently bears a new relation to the six others. Next to the phenomenon of seven sounds perpetually circulating in a geometrical progression, according to the length of the strings or the number of their vibrations, every ear must be sensible, that two of the seven intervals in the complete series, or octave, whether we consider it as placed in a circular form, or in a right line with the first sound repeated, are much shorter than the five other intervals; and on these two phenomena the modes of the *Hindus* (who seem ignorant of our complicated harmony) are principally constructed. The longer intervals we shall call *tones*, and the shorter (in compliance with custom) *semitones*, without mentioning their exact ratios; and it is evident that, as the *places* of the semitones admit *seven* variations relative to one fundamental sound, there are as many modes, which may be called *primary;* but we must not confound them with our modern modes, which result from the system of accords now established in *Europe*: they may rather be compared with those of the *Roman* Church, where some valuable remnants of old Grecian musick are preserved in the sweet, majestick, simple, and affecting strains of the Plain Song. Now, since each of the tones may be divided, we find *twelve* semitones in the whole series; and, since each semitone may in its turn become the leader of a series formed after the model of every primary mode, we have *seven* times *twelve*, or *eighty-four*, modes in all, of which *seventy-seven* may be named *secondary;* and we shall see accordingly that the *Persians* and the *Hindus* (at least in their most popular system) have exactly *eighty-four* modes, though distinguished by different appellations and arranged in different classes; but, since many of them are unpleasing to the ear, others difficult in execution, and few sufficiently marked by a character of sentiment and expression, which the higher musick always requires, the genius of the *Indians* has enabled them to retain the *number* of modes, which nature seems to have indicated, and to give each of them a character of its own by a happy and beautiful contrivance. Why any one series of sounds, the ratios of which are ascertained by observation and expressible by figures, should have a peculiar effect on the organ of hearing, and, by the auditory nerves, on the mind, will then only be known by mortals, when they shall know why each of the seven colours in the rainbow, where a proportion, analogous to that of musical sounds, most wonderfully, prevails, has a certain specifick effect on our eyes; why the shades of green and blue, for instance, are soft and soothing, while those of red and yellow distress and dazzle the sight; but, without striving to account for the phenomena, let us be satisfied with knowing, that some of the *modes* have distinct perceptible properties, and may be applied to the expression of various mental emotions; a fact, which ought well to be considered by those performers, who would reduce them all to a dull uniformity, and sacrifice the true beauties of their art to an injudicious temperament.

The ancient *Greeks*, among whom this delightful art was long in the hands of poets, and of mathematicians, who had much less to do with it, ascribe almost all its magick to the diversity of their *Modes*, but have left us little more than the names of them, without such discriminations, as might have enabled us to compare them with their own, and apply them to practice: their writers addressed themselves to *Greeks*, who could not but know their national musick; and most of those writers were professed men of science, who thought more of calculating ratios than of inventing melody; so that, whenever we speak of the soft *Eolian* mode, of the tender *Lydian*, the voluptuous *Ionick*, the manly *Dorian*, or the animating *Phrygian*, we use mere phrases, I believe, without clear ideas. For all that is known concerning the musick of *Greece*, let me refer those, who have no inclination to read the dry works of the *Greeks* themselves, to a little tract of the learned WALLIS, which he printed as an appendix to the Harmonicks of PTOLEMY, to the "Dictionary of Musick" by ROUSSEAU, whose pen, formed 'to elucidate all the arts, had the property of spreading light before it on the darkest subjects, as if he had written with phosphorus on the sides of a cavern; and, lastly, to the dissertation of Dr. BURNEY, who passing slightly over all that is obscure, explains with perspicuity whatever is explicable, and gives dignity to the character of a modern musician, by uniting it with that of a scholar and philosopher.

The unexampled felicity of our nation, who diffuse the blessings of a mild government over the finest part of *India*, would enable us to attain a perfect knowledge of the oriental musick, which is known and practised in these *British* dominions not by mercenary performers only, but even by *Muselmans* and *Hindus* of eminent rank and learning: a native of *Cáshán*, lately resident at *Murshedábad*, had a complete acquaintance with the *Persian* theory and practice; and the best artists in *Hindustan* would cheerfully attend our concerts: we have an easy access to approved *Asiatick* treatises on musical composition, and need not lament with CHARDIN, that he neglected to procure at *Isfahán* the explanation of a small tract on that subject, which he carried to *Europe:* we may here examine the best instruments of *Asia*, may be masters of them, if we please, or at least may compare them with ours: the concurrent labours, or rather amusements, of several in our own body, may facilitate the attainment of correct ideas on a subject so delightfully interesting; and a free communication from time to time of their respective discoveries would conduct them more surely and speedily, as well as more agreeably, to their desired end. Such would be the advantages of union, or, to borrow a term from the art before us, of *harmonious accord*, in all our pursuits, and above all in that of knowledge.

On *Persian* musick, which is not the subject of this paper, it would be improper to enlarge: the whole system of it is explained in a celebrated collection of tracts on pure and mixed mathematicks, entitled *Durratu'ltáj*, and composed by a very learned man, so generally called *Allámi Shírazí*, or the *great philosopher* of *Shíráz;* that his proper name is almost forgotten; but, as the modern *Persians* had access, I believe, to PTOLEMY'S harmonicks, their mathematical writers on musick treat it rather as a science than as an art, and seem, like the *Greeks*, to be more intent on splitting tones into quarters and eighth parts, of which they compute the ratios to show their arithmetick, than on displaying the principles of modulation as it may affect the passions. I apply the same observation to a short, but masterly, tract of the famed ABU'SI'NA, and suspect that it is applicable to an elegant essay in *Persian*, called *Shamsu'láswát*, of which I have not had courage to read more than the preface. It will be sufficient to subjoin on this head, that the *Persians* distribute their *eighty-four* modes, according to an idea of locality, into twelve *rooms*, twenty-four *recesses*, and forty-eight *angles* or *corners* : in the beautiful tale known by the title of the *Four Dervises*, originally written in *Persia* with great purity and elegance, we find the description of a concert, where your singers, with as many different instruments, are represented " *modulating* in twelve *makáms* or *perdahs*, twenty-four *shóbahs*, and forty-eight *gúshahs*, and beginning a mirthful song of HA'FIZ on vernal delight in the *perdah* named *rást*, or direct." All the twelve *perdahs*, with their appropriated *shóbahs*, are enumerated by AMI'N, a writer and musician of *Hindustán*, who mentions an opinion of the learned, that only *seven* primary modes were in use before the reign of PARVI'Z, whose musical entertainments are magnificently described by the incomparable NIZA'MI : the modes are chiefly denominated like those of the *Greeks* and *Hindus*, from different regions or towns ; as, among the *perdahs*, we see *Hijás*, *Irák*, *Isfahán* : and, among the *shóbahs*, or secondary modes, *Zábul*, *Níshápùr*, and the like. In a *Sanscrit* book, which shall soon be particularly mentioned, I find the scale of a mode, named *Hijéja*, specified in the following verse :

Máns'agraha sa nyásò' c'hilò bijéjastu sáyáhnè.

The name of this mode is not *Indian;* and, if I am

right in believing it a corruption of *Hijáz*, which could hardly be written otherwise in the *Nágari* letters, we must conclude that it was imported from *Persia*: we have discovered then a *Persian* or *Arabian* mode with this diapason :

D, E, F sharp, G sharp, A, B, C sharp, D; where the first semitone appears between the *fourth* and *fifth* notes, and the second between the *seventh* and *eighth*; as in the natural scale, *fa, sol, la, si, ut, re, mi, fa* : but the C sharp and G sharp, or *ga* and *ni* of the *Indian* author, are variously *changed*, and probably the series may be formed in a manner not very different (though certainly there is a diversity) from our major mode of D. This melody must necessarily end with the *fifth* note from the tonick and begin with the tonick itself; and it would be a gross violation of musical decorum in *India*, to sing it at any time except at the close of day : these rules are comprized in the verse above-cited; but the species of octave is arranged according to Mr. FOWKE'S remarks on the *Viná*, compared with the fixed *Swaragráma*, or gamut, of all the *Hindu* musicians.

Let us proceed to the *Indian* system, which is minutely explained in a great number of *Sanscrit* books, by authors, who leave arithmetick and geometry to their astronomers, and properly discourse on musick

as an art confined to the pleasures of imagination.
The *Pandits* of this province unanimously prefer the
Dámódara to any of the popular *Sangítas*; but I have
not been able to procure a good copy of it, and am
perfectly satisfied with the *Nárayan*, which I received
from *Benáres*, and in which the *Dámódara* is frequently quoted. The *Persian* book, entitled *a Present from India*, was composed, under the patronage
of AAZEM SHA'H, by the very diligent and ingenious MIRZA' KHA'N, and contains a minute account of *Hindu* literature in all, or most of, its
branches: he professes to have extracted his elaborate chapter on musick, with the assistance of *Pandits*, from the *Rágárnava*, or "Sea of Passions," the
Rágáderpana, or "Mirror of Modes," the *Sabhávinóda*,
or "Delight of Assemblies," and some other approved
treatises in *Sanscrit*. The *Sangitaderpan*, which he
also names among his authorities, has been translated into *Persian*; but my experience justifies me
in pronouncing, that the *Moghols* have no idea of
accurate *translation*, and give that name to a mixture
of gloss and text with a flimsy paraphrase of them
both; that they are wholly unable, yet always pretend, to write *Sanscrit* words in *Arabick* letters; that
a man, who knows the *Hindus* only from *Persian*
books, does not know the *Hindus*; and that an *European*, who follows the muddy rivulets of *Muselman*

writers on *India*, instead of drinking from the pure fountain of *Hindu* learning, will be in perpetual danger of misleading himself and others. From the just severity of this. censure, I except neither ABU'LFAZL, nor his brother FAIZI, nor MOHSANI FA"NI, nor MIRZA' KHA'N himself; and I speak of all four after an attentive perusal of their works. A tract on musick in the idiom of *Mathurà*, with several essays in pure *Hindustàni*, lately passed through my hands; and I possess a dissertation on the same art in the soft dialect of *Panjáb*, or *Panchanada*, where the national melody has, I am told, a peculiar and striking character; but I am very little acquainted with those dialects, and persuade myself, that nothing has been written in them, which may not be found more copiously and beautifully expressed in the *language*, as the *Hindus* perpetually call it, *of the Gods*, that is of their ancient bards, philosophers and legislators.

The most valuable work, that I have seen, and perhaps the most valuable that exists, on the subject of Indian musick, is named *Rágavibódha*, or *The Doctrine of Musical Modes*; and it ought here to be mentioned very particularly, because none of the *Pandits*, in our provinces, nor any of those from *Cási* or *Cashmir*, to whom I have shown it, appear to have known that it was extant; and it may be considered

as a treasure in the history of the art, which the zeal
of Colonel POLIER has brought into light, and
perhaps has preserved from destruction. He had
purchased, among other curiosities, a volume containing a number of separate essays on musick in
prose and verse, and in a great variety of idioms:
besides tracts in *Arabick*, *Hindi* and *Persian*, it includes a short essay in *Latin* by ALSTEDIUS, with
an interlineary *Persian* translation, in which the passages quoted from LUCRETIUS and VIRGIL
made a singular appearance; but the brightest gem
in the string was the *Rágavibódha*, which the Colonel
permitted my *Nágari* writer to transcribe, and the
transcript was diligently collated with the original
by my *Pandit* and myself. It seems a very ancient
composition, but is less old unquestionably than the
Ratnacára by SA'RNGA DE'VA, which is more than
once mentioned in it, and a copy of which Mr. Bur-
row procured in his journey to *Heridwar*: the name
of the author was SO'MA, and he appears to have
been a practical musician as well as a great scholar
and an elegant poet; for the whole book, without
excepting the strains noted in letters, which fill the
fifth and last chapter of it, consists of masterly
couplets in the melodious metre called *A'ryà*; the
first, third, and *fourth* chapters explain the doctrine
of musical sounds, their division and succession, the

variations of scales by temperament, and the enumeration of modes on a system totally different from
those, which will presently be mentioned; and the
second chapter contains a minute description of different *Vínás* with rules for playing on them. This
book alone would enable me, were I master of my
time, to compose a treatise on the musick of *India,*
with assistance, in the practical part, from an *European* professor and a native player on the *Víná*; but
I have leisure only to present you with an essay, and
even that, I am conscious, must be very superficial :
it may be sometimes, but, I trust, not often, erroneous; and I have spared no pains to secure myself
from error.

In the literature of the *Hindus* all nature is animated and personified; every fine art is declared to
have been revealed from heaven; and all knowledge,
divine and human, is traced to its source in the
Védas; among which the *Sámavéda* was intended to
be *sung,* whence the reader or singer of it is called
Udgátri or *Sámaga*; in Colonel POLIER'S copy of
it the strains are noted in figures, which it may not
be impossible to decypher. On account of this distinction, say the *Bráhmens,* the supreme preserving
power, in the form of CRISHNA, having enumerated in the *Gítà* various orders of beings, to the chief
of which he compares himself, pronounces, that

"*among the* Védas *he was the* Sáman." From that *Véda* was accordingly derived the *Upavéda* of the *Gandharbas*, or musicians in INDRA'S heaven; so that the divine art was communicated to our species by BRAHMA himself or by his *active power* SERESWATI, the Goddess of Speech; and their mythological son NA'RED, who was in truth an ancient law-giver and astronomer, invented the *Viná*, called also *Cach'hapí*, or *Testudo*; a very remarkable fact, which may be added to the other proofs of a resemblance between that *Indian* God, and the MERCURY of the *Latians*. Among inspired mortals the first musicians is believed to have been the sage BHERAT, who was the inventor, they say, of *Nátacs*, or dramas represented with songs and dances, and author of a musical system which bears his name. If we can rely on MIRZA' KHA'N, there are four principal *Matas*, or systems, the first of which is ascribed to ISWARA, or OSIRIS; the second to BHERAT; the third to HANUMAT, or P'A'VAN, the PAN of India, supposed to be the son of PAVANA, the regent of air; and the fourth to CALLINA'T'H, a *Rìshi*, or *Indian* philosopher, eminently skilled in musick, theoretical and practical: all four are mentioned by SO'MA; and it is the *third* of them, which must be very ancient, and seems to have been extremely popular, that I propose to explain after a few introductory remarks; but I may here observe with SO'MA, who exhibits a system of his own, and with the author of the *Náráyan*, who mentions a great many others, that almost every kingdom and province had a peculiar style of melody, and very different names for the modes, as well as a different arrangement and enumeration of them.

The two phenomena, which have already been stated as the foundation of musical modes, could not long have escaped the attention of the *Hindus*, and their flexible language readily supplied them with names for the seven *Swaras*, or sounds, which they dispose in the following order: *Shádja*, pronounced *Sharja*, *Rìshabha*, *Gándhára*, *Madhyama*, *Panchama*, *Dhaivata*, *Nisháda*, but the first of them is emphatically named *Swara*, or the *sound*, from the important office, which it bears in the scale; and hence, by taking the seven *initial letters* or syllables of those words, they contrived a notation for their airs and at the same time exhibited a gamut, at least as convenient as that of GUIDO: they call it *Swaragráma* or *Septaca*, and express it in this form:

Sa, ri, ga, ma, pa, dha, ni,

three of which syllables are, by a singular concurrence exactly the same, though not all in the same places, with three of those invented by DAVID

MOSTARE, as a substitute for the troublesome gamut used in his time, and which he arranges thus :

Bo, ce, di, ga, lo, ma, ni.

As to the notation of melody, since every *Indian* consonant includes by its nature the short vowel *a*, five of the sounds are denoted by single consonants, and the two others have different short vowels taken from their full names; by substituting long vowels, the *time* of each note is doubled, and other marks are used for a farther elongation of them; the octaves above and below the mean scale, the connection and acceleration of notes, the graces of execution or manners of fingering the instrument, are expressed very clearly by small circles and ellipses, by little chains, by curves, by straight lines, horizontal or perpendicular, and by crescents, all in various positions: the close of a strain is distinguished by a lotos-flower; but the time and measure are determined by the prosody of the verse and by the comparative length of each syllable, with which every note or assemblage of notes respectively corresponds. If I understand the native musicians, they have not only the *chromatick*, but even the second or new *enharmonick*, genus; for they unanimously reckon twenty-two *s'rutis*, or quarters and thirds of a tone, in their octave: they do not pretend that those minute intervals

are mathematically equal, but consider them as equal
in practice, and allot them to the several notes in
the following order: to *sa*, *ma*, and *pa*, four; to *ri*
and *dha*, three; to *ga* and *ni*, two; giving very
smooth and significant names to each *s'ruti*. Their
original scale therefore stands thus:

Sa,	ri,	ga,	ma,	pa,	dha,	ni,	sa,
4s'	3s'	2s'	4s'	4s'	3s'	2s'	

The semitones accordingly are placed as in our
diatonick scale: the intervals between the fourth and
fifth, and between the first and second, are major
tones; but that between the fifth and sixth, which is
minor in our scale, appears to be major in theirs;
and the two scales are made to coincide by taking a
s'ruti from *pa* and adding it to *dha*, or, in the language of *Indian* artists, by raising *Servaretnà* to the
class of *Sántà* and her sisters; for every *s'ruti* they
consider as a little nymph, and the nymphs of *Panchama*, or the *fifth* note, are *Málinì, Chapalá, Lôlá,*
and *Servaretnà,* while *Sántà* and her two sisters regularly belong to *Dhaivata*: such at least is the system of CO'HALA, one of the ancient bards, who has
left a treatise on musick.

SO'MA seems to admit that a quarter or third of a
tone cannot be separately and distinctly heard from

the *Vína*; but he takes for granted, that its effect is
very perceptible in their arrangement of modes; and
their sixth. I imagine, is almost universally diminished by one *s'ruti;* for he only mentions two modes,
in which all the seven notes are *unaltered*. I tried in
vain to discover any difference in practice between
the *Indian* scale, and that of our own; but, knowing
my ear to be insufficiently exercised, I requested a
German professor of musick to accompany with his
violin a *Hindu* lutanist, who sung *by note* some popular airs on the loves of CRISHNA and RA'DHA*;
he assured me, that the scales were the same; and Mr.
SHORE afterwards informed me, that, when the
voice of a native singer was in tune with his harpsichord, he found the *Hindu* series of seven notes to
ascend, like ours, by a sharp third.

For the construction and character of the *Vínà*, I
must refer you to the very accurate and valuable
paper of Mr. FOWKE† in the first volume of your
Transactions; and I now exhibit a scale of its fingerboard, which I received from him with the drawing
of the instrument, and on the correctness of which

---

* See reference to Krishna and Rádhá on pages 26, 105
and 129.

† See reference to Francis Fowke's description of the
víná on pages 33 and 34.

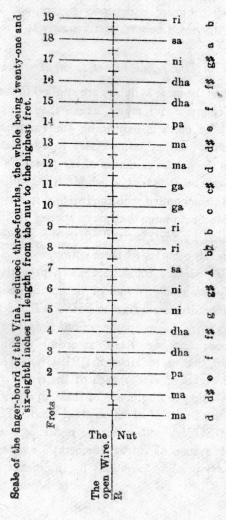

Scale of the finger-board of the Vínā, reduced three-fourths, the whole being twenty-one and six-eighth inches in length, from the nut to the highest fret.

Frets		
19	ri	b
18	sa	a
17	ni	g♯ a♯
16	dha	f♯
15	dha	f
14	pa	e
13	ma	d♯
12	ma	d
11	ga	c♯
10	ga	c
9	ri	b
8	ri	b♭
7	sa	A
6	ni	g♯
5	ni	g
4	dha	f♯
3	dha	f
2	pa	e
1	ma	d♯
	ma	d

The Nut

The open Wire.

you may confidently depend; the regular *Indian*
gamut answers, I believe, pretty nearly to our major
mode:

Ut, re, mi, fa, sol, la, si, ut,

and, when the same syllables are applied to the notes,
which compose our minor mode, they are distinguished by epithets expressing the change, which
they suffer. It may be necessary to add, before we
come to the *Rágas,* or modes of the *Hindus,* that the
twenty-one *murch'hanas,* which Mr. SHORE'S native
musician confounded with the two and twenty *s'rutis,*
appear to be no more than *seven* species of diapason
multiplied by *three,* according to the difference of
pitch in the compass of three octaves.

RAGA, which I translate a *mode,* properly signi-
fies a *passion* or *affection* of the mind, each mode
being intended, according to BHERAT'S definition
of it, to move one or another of our simple or mixed
affections; and we learn accordingly from the
Náráyan, that, in the days of CRISHNA, there were
sixteen thousand modes, each of the *Gópìs* at *Mat'-
hura* choosing to sing in one of them, in order to captivate the heart of their pastoral God. The very
learned SO'MA, who mixes no mythology with his
accurate system of *Rágas,* enumerates *nine hundred
and sixty* possible variations by the means of tem-

perament, but selects from them, as applicable to practice, only *twenty-three* primary modes, from which he deduces many others; although he allows, that by a diversity of ornament and by various contrivances, the *Rágas* might, like the waves of the sea, be multiplied to an infinite number. We have already observed, that *eighty-four modes* or *manners* might naturally be formed by giving the lead to each of our *twelve* sounds, and varying in *seven* different ways the position of the semitones; but, since many of those modes would be insufferable in practice, and some would have no character sufficiently marked, the *Indians* appear to have retained with predilection the number indicated by nature, and to have enforced their system by two powerful aids, the *association of ideas* and the *mutilation of the regular scales.*

Whether it had occurred to the *Hindu* musicians, that the velocity or slowness of sounds must depend, in a certain ratio, upon the rarefaction and condensation of the air, so that their motion must be quicker in summer than in spring or autumn, and much quicker than in winter, I cannot assure myself; but am persuaded, that their primary modes, in the system ascribed to PA'VAN, were first arranged according to the number of *Indian* seasons.

The year is distributed by the *Hindus* into six *ritus*, or seasons, each consisting of two months; and

the first season according to the *Amarcósha*, began
with *Márgas'irsha*, near the time of the winter sol-
stice, to which month accordingly we see CRISHNA
compared in the *Gítá*; but the old lunar year began,
I believe, with *A'swina*, or near the autumnal equinox,
when the moon was at the full in the first mansion :
hence the musical season, which takes the lead, includes the months of *A'swin* and *Cártic*, and bears
the name of *Sarad*, corresponding with part of our
autumn; the next in order are *Hémanta* and *Sisira*,
derived from words, which signify *frost* and *dew;*
then come *Vasanta*, or spring, called also *Surabhi* or
fragrant, and *Pushpasamaya*, or the flower time;
Gríshma, or heat; and *Vershà*, or the season of rain.
By appropriating a different mode to each of the
different seasons, the artists of *India* connected certain strains with certain ideas, and were able to recall the memory of autumnal merriment at the close
of the harvest, or of separation and melancholy (very
different from our ideas at *Calcutta*) during the cold
months; of reviving hilarity on the appearance of
blossoms, and complete vernal delight in the month
of *Madhu* or *honey*; of languor during the dry heats,
and of refreshment by the first rains, which cause in
this climate a second spring. Yet farther: since
the lunar year, by which festivals and superstitious
duties are constantly regulated, proceeds concur-

rently with the solar year, to which the seasons are
necessarily referred, *devotion* comes also to the aid
of musick, and all the *powers of nature*, which are
allegorically worshipped as gods and goddesses on
their several holidays, contribute to the influence of
song on minds naturally susceptible of religious emotions. Hence it was, I imagine, that PA'VAN, or the
inventor of his musical system, reduced the number
of original modes from *seven* to *six;* but even this
was not enough for his purpose; and he had recourse
to the *five* principal divisions of the day, which are
the *morning, noon* and *evening,* called *trisandhya,*
with the two intervals between them, or the *forenoon*
and *afternoon*: by adding *two* divisions, or intervals, of the night, and by leaving one species of
melody without any such restriction, SO'MA reckons
eight variations in respect of time; and the system
of PA'VAN retains that number also in the second
order of derivative modes. Every branch of knowledge in this country has been embellished by poetical fables; and the inventive talents of the *Greeks*
never suggested a more charming allegory than the
lovely families of the six *Rágas,* named, in the order
of seasons above exhibited, *BHAIRAVA, MA'LAVA,*
SRI'RA'GA, HINDO'LA or VASANTA, DI'PACA,
and ME'GHA; each of whom is a Genius, or Demi-
god, wedded to five *Ráginis,* or Nymphs, and father

of *eight* little Genii, called his *Putras*, or sons; the fancy of SHAKSPEAR and the pencil of ALBANO might have been finely employed in giving speech and form to this assemblage of new aërial beings, who people the fairy-land of *Indian* imagination; nor have the *Hindu* poets and painters lost the advantages, with which so beautiful a subject presented them. A whole chapter of the *Náráyan* contains descriptions of the *Rágas* and their consorts, extracted chiefly from the *Dámódara*, the *Caláncura*, the *Retnamálá*, the *Chandricà*, and a metrical tract on musick ascribed to the God NA'RED himself, from which, as among so many beauties a particular selection would be very perplexing, I present you with the first that occurs, and have no doubt, that you will think the *Sanscrit* language equal to *Italian* in softness and elegance.

> Lílá viháréna vanántarálé,
> Chinvan prasúnáni vadhú saháyah,
> Vilási vesódita divya múrtıh,
> Srîrága ésha prat'hitah prit'hivyám.

"The demigod SRI'RA'GA, famed over all this earth, sweetly sports with his nymphs, gathering fresh blossoms in the bosom of yon grove; and his divine lineaments are distinguished through his graceful vesture."

These and similar images, but wonderfully diversified, are expressed in a variety of measures, and represented by delicate pencils in the *Rágamálas*, which all of us have examined, and among which the most beautiful are in the possession of Mr. R. JOHNSON and Mr. HAY. A noble work might be composed by any musician and scholar, who enjoyed leisure and disregarded expense, if he would exhibit a perfect system of *Indian* musick from *Sanscrit* authorities, with the old melodies of SO'MA applied to the scngs of JAYADE'VA, embellished with descriptions of all the modes accurately translated, and with Mr. HAY'S *Rágamálà* delineated and engraved by the scholars of CIPRIANI and BARTOLOZZI.

Let us proceed to the second artifice of the *Hindu* musicians, in giving their modes a distinct character and a very agreeable diversity of expression. A curious passage from PLUTARCH'S "Treatise on Musick" is translated and explained by Dr. BURNEY, and stands as the text of the most interesting chapter in his dissertation: since I cannot procure the original I exhibit a paraphrase of his translation, on the correctness of which I can rely; but I have avoided, as much as possible, the technical words of the *Greeks*, which it might be necessary to explain at some length. "We are informed, says PLUTARCH, by ARISTOXENUS, that musicians ascribe to OLYMPUS of *Mysia* the invention of *enharmonick* melody, and conjecture, that, when he was playing diatonically on his flute, and frequently passed from the highest of four sounds to the lowest but one, or conversely, skipping over the second in descent, or the third in ascent, of that series, he perceived a singular beauty of expression, which induced him to dispose the whole series of seven or eight sounds by similar skips, and to frame by the same analogy his *Dorian* mode, omitting every sound *peculiar* to the diatonick and chromatick melodies then in use, but without adding any that have since been made essential to the *new* enharmonick: in this genus, they say, he composed the Nome, or strain, called *Spondean*, because it was used in temples at the time of religious *libations*. Those, it seems were the *first* enharmonick melodies; and are still retained by some, who play on the flute in the antique style without any division of a semitone; for it was after the age of OLYMPUS, that the quarter of a tone was admitted into the *Lydian* and *Phrygian* modes; and it was he, therefore, who, by introducing an exquisite melody before unknown in *Greece*, became the author and parent of the most beautiful and affecting musick."

This method then of adding to the character and effect of a mode by diminishing the number of its primitive sounds, was introduced by a *Greek* of the lower *Asia*, who flourished, according to the learned and accurate writer of the Travels of ANACHARSIS, about the middle of the *thirteenth* century before CHRIST; but it must have been older still among the HINDUS, if the system, to which I now return, was actually invented in the age of RA'MA.

Since it appears from the *Náráyan*, that *thirty-six* modes are in general use, and the rest very rarely applied to practice, I shall exhibit only the scales of the six *Rágas* and thirty *Ráginis*, according to SO'MA, the authors quoted in the *Náráyan*, and the books explained by *Pandits* to MIRZA'KHA'N, on whose credit I must rely for that of *Cacubhá*, which I cannot find in my *Sanscrit* treatises on musick: had I depended on him for information of greater consequence, he would have led me into a very serious mistake; for he asserts, what I now find erroneous, that the *graha* is the first note of every mode, with which every song, that is composed in it, must invariably begin *and end*. Three distinguished sounds in each mode are called *graha*, *nyása*, *ans'a*, and the writer of the *Náráyan* defines them in the two following couplets.

Graha swarah sa ityuctó yó gítádau samarpitah,
Nyása swarastu sa próctó yó gítádi samápticah:

Yó vyactivyanjacó gánè, yasya servé'nugáminah,
Yasya servatra báhulyam vády ans'ó pi nrīpótamah.

"The note, called *graha*, is placed at the beginning, and that named *nyása*, at the end, of a song;
that note, which displays the peculiar melody, and
to which all the others are subordinate, that, which
is always of the greatest use, is like a sovereign,
though a mere *ans'a*, or portion."

"By the word *vádi*," says the commentator, "he
means the note, which announces and ascertains the
Rága, and which may be considered as the present
origin of the *graha* and *nyása*," this clearly shows, I
think, that the *ans'a* must be the tonick; and we shall
find, that the two other notes are generally its third
and fifth, or the mediant and the dominant. In the
poem entitled *Mágha* there is a musical simile, which
may illustrate and confirm our idea.

Analpatwát pradhánatwád ans'asyévétaraswaráh,
Vijigíshórnripatayah prayánti pericháratam.

"From the greatness, from the transcendant
qualities, of that Heró eager for conquest, other
kings march in subordination to him, as other notes
are subordinate to the *ans'a*."

If the *ans'a* be the tonick, or modal note, of the
Hindus, we may confidently exhibit the scales of the

Indian modes, according to SO'MA, denoting by an asterisk the omission of a note.

BHAIRAVA: dha, *ni*, sa, ri, *ga*, ma, pa.
Varáti: sa, ri, *ga*, *ma*, pa, dha, *ni*.
Medhyamádi: ma, pa, *, *ni*, sa, * *ga*.
Bhairavi: sa, *ri*, ga, ma, *pa*, dha, ni.
Saindhaví: sa, *ri*, *, ma, pa, *dha*, *.
Bengáli: *sa*, ri, *ga*, ma, pa, dha, *ni*.

MA'LAVA: *ni*, sa, ri, *ga*, ma, pa, dha.
Tô'dì: *ga*, ma, pa, dha, *ni*, sa, ri.
Gau'di: *ni*, sa, ri, *, ma, pa, *.
Góndàcrì: sa, ri, *ga*, ma, pa, *, *ni*.
Susťhávatì: not in SO'MA.
Cacubhà: not in SO'MA.

SRI'RA'GA: *ni*, sa, *ri*, *ga*, ma, pa, *dha*.
Málavas'rì: sa, *, *ga*, ma, pa, *, *ni*.
Máraví: *ga*, ma, pa, *, *ni*, sa, *.
Dhanyásì: sa, *, *ga*, ma, pa,* *ni*.
Vasantì, sa, ri, *ga*, ma, *, dha, *ni*.
Asáverì: ma, pa, dha, *ni*, sa. ri, *ga*.

HINDO'LA: ma, *, dha, *ni*, sa, * *ga*.
Rámacrì: sa, ri, *ga*, ma, pa, dha, *ni*.
Dês'ácshì: *ga*, ma, pa, *dha*, *, sa, *ri*.
Lelità: sa, ri, *ga*, ma, *, dha, *ni*.
Vélávalì: dha, *ni*, sa, *, *ga*, ma, *.
Patamanjarì: not in SO'MA.

DI'PACA: not in SO'MA.
Dés'i: ri, *, *ma*, pa, dha, *ni*, sa.
Cámbódì: sa, *ri*, *ga*, ma, pa, *dha*, *.
Nettà: sa, *ri*, *ga*, ma, pa, *dha*, *ni*.
Cédárì: *ni*, sa, *ri*, *ga*, ma, pa, dha.
Carnátì: *ni*, sa, *, *ga*, ma, pa, *.

ME'GHA: not in SO'MA.
Taccà: sa, ri, *ga*, ma, pa, dha, *ni*.
Mellárì: *dha*, *, sa, *ri*, *, ma, pa.
Gurjarì: ri, *ga*, ma, *, dha, *ni*, sa.
Bhúpálì: *ga*, *, pa, *dha*, *, sa, *ri*.
Désacrì: sa, ri, ga, *ma*, *pa*, dha, *ni*.

It is impossible, that I should have erred much, if at all, in the preceding table, because the regularity of the *Sanscrit* metre has in general enabled me to correct the manuscript; but I have some doubt as to *Vélávalì*, of which *pa* is declared to be the *ans'a*, or tonick, though it is said in the same line, that both *pa* and *ri* may be omitted. I therefore, have supposed *dha* to be the true reading, both MIRZA'-KHA'N and the *Náráyan* exhibiting that note as the leader of the mode. The notes printed in *Italick* letters are variously *changed* by temperament or by shakes and other graces; but, even if I were able to give you in words a distinct notion of those changes, the account of each mode would be insufferably tedious, and scarce intelligible without the assistance of a masterly performer on the *Indian* lyre. According to the best authorities adduced in the *Náráyan*, the thirty-six modes are, in some provinces, arranged in these forms.

BHAIRAVA: dha, ni, sa, ri, *ga*, ma, pa.
Varátì: sa, ri, ga, ma, *pa*, dha, ni.
Medhyamádi: ni, sa, *, ga, ma, pa, dha.
Bhairavì: sa, *, ga, ma, *, dha, ni.
Saindhavì: pa, dha, ni, sa, ri, ga, ma.
Bengálì: sa, ri, *ga*, ma, pa, dha, ni.

MA'LAVA: ma, *, dha, ni, sa, ri, ga.
Tô'di: ma, pa, dha, ni, sa, ri, ga.
Gau'dì: ni, sa, ri, ga, ma, *, dha.
Góndacrì: sa, *, ga, ma, pa, *, ni.
Sust'hávatì: dha, *ni*, *sa*, ri, ga, ma, *.
Cacubhā: not in the *Náráyan*.

SRI'RA'GA: sa, ri, ga, ma, *pa*, dha, ni.
Málavas'rì: sa, *ri*, ga, ma, pa, *dha*, ni.
Máravì: sa, *, ga, ma, pa, dha, ni.
Dhanyásì: sa, ri, ga, *ma*, pa, dha, ni.
Vasantì: sa, ri, ga, ma, pa, dha, ni.
Asáverì: ri, ga, ma, pa, dha, ni, sa.

HINDO'LA : sa, *, ga, ma, *, dha, ni.
Rámacrì : sa, *ri,* ga, ma, pa, dha, ni.
Dés'ácshì : ga, ma, pa, dha, ni, sa, *.
Lelità : sa, *, ga, ma, pa, *, ni.
Vélávalì : dha, ni, *sa,* ri, ga, ma, pa.
Patamanjarì : pa, *dha,* ni, sa, *ri, ga,* ma.

DI'PACA : omitted.
Dés'i : ni, sa, ri, ga, ma, pa, dha.
Cámbódì : sa, ri, ga, ma, pa, dha, *ni.*
Nettà : sa, *ri,* ga, ma, pa, dha, ni.
Cédárì : omitted.
Carnátì : ni, sa, ri, ga, ma, pa, dha.

ME'GHA : dha, ni, sa, ri, ga, ma, pa.
Taccà : (a mixed mode).
Mellárì : dha, ni, *, ri, ga, ma, *.
Gurjarì : omitted in the *Náráyan.*
Bhúpálì : sa, ri, ga, *, pa, dha, *.
Désacrì : ni, sa, *, ga, ma, pa, *.

Among the scales just enumerated we may safely
ıx on that of SRI'RA'GA for our own major mode,
since its form and character are thus described in a
Sanscrit couplet.

Játinyásagrahagrámáns'éshu sha'djò, *lpapanchamah,*
Sringáravírayorjnéyah *Srîrágò* gítacóvidaiah,

" Musicians know *Srî'râ'ga* to have *sa* for its principal note and the first of its scale, with *pa* diminished, and to be used for expressing heroick love and valour." Now the diminution of *pa* by one *s'ruti* gives us the modern *European* scale,

ut, re, mi, fa, sol, la, si, ut,

with a minor tone, or, as the *Indians* would express it, with three *s'rutis*, between the fifth and sixth notes.

On the formulas exhibited by MIRZA' KHA'N I have less reliance; but, since he professes to give them from *Sanscrit* authorities, it seemed proper to transcribe them.

BHAIRAVA: dha, ni, sa, *, ga, ma, *.
Varáti : sa, ri, ga, ma, pa, dha, ni.
Medhyamádi : ma, pa, dha, ni, sa, ri, ga.
Bhairavî : ma, pa, dha, ni, sa, ri, ga.
Saindhavì : sa, ri, ga, ma, pa, dha, ni.
Bengálì : sa, ri, ga, ma, pa, dha, ni.

MA'LAVA: sa, ri, ga, ma, pa, dha, ni.
Tô'dì : sa, ri, ga, ma, pa, dha, ni.
Gau'dì : sa, *, ga, ma, *, dha, ni.
Gôndacrì : ni, sa, *, ga, ma, pa, *.
Sust'hávatì : dha, ni, sa, ri, ga, ma, *.
Cacubhà : dha, ni, sa, ri, ga, ma, pa.

SRI'RA'GA : sa, ri, ga, ma, pa, dha, ni.
Malavas'rì : sa, ri, ga, ma, pa, dha, ni.
Máravì : sa, *, pa, ga, ma, dha, ni.
Dhanyásì : sa, pa, dha, ni, ri, ga, *.
Vasantì : sa, ri, ga, ma, pa, dha, ni.
Asáverì : dha, ni, sa, *, *, ma, pa.

HINDO'LA : sa, *, ga, ma, pa, *, ni.
Rámacrì : sa, *, ga, ma, pa, *, ni.
Dés'ácshì : ga, ma, pa, dha, ni, sa, *.
Lelità : dha, ni, sa, *, ga, ma, *.
Vélavalì : dha, ni, sa, ri, ga, ma, pa.
Patamanjarì : pa, dha, ni, sa, ri, ga, ma.

DI'PACA : sa, ri, ga, ma, pa, dha, ni.
Dés'ì : ri, ga, ma, *, dha, ni, sa.
Cámbódi : dha, ni, sa, ri, ga, ma, pa.
Nettà : sa, ni, *, dha, pa, ma, ga, ri.
Cédarì : ni, sa, *, ga, ma, pa, *.
Carnátì : ni, sa, ri, ga, ma, pa, *, dha.

ME'GHA : dha, ni, sa, ri, ga, *, *.
Taccà : sa, ri, ga, ma, pa, dha, ni.
Mellárì : dha, ni, *, ri, ga, ma, *.
Gurjarì : ri, ga, ma, pa, dha, ni, sa.
Bhúpálì : sa, ga, ma, dha, ni, pa, ri.
Désacrì : sa, ri, ga, ma, pa, dha, ni.

It may reasonably be suspected, that the *Moghol* writer could not have shown the distinction, which must necessarily have been made, between the different modes, to which he assigns the same formula; and, as to his inversions of the notes in some of the *Ráginis*, I can only say, that no such changes appear in the *Sanscrit* books, which I have inspected. I leave our scholars and musicians to find, among the scales here exhibited, the *Dorian* mode of OLYMPUS; but it cannot escape notice, that the *Chinese* scale, C, D, E, *, G, A, *, corresponds very nearly with *ga, ma,* pa, *, ni, sa, *, or the *Máraví* of SO'MA : we have long known in *Bengal,* from the information of a *Scotch* gentleman skilled in musick, that the wild, but charming melodies of the ancient highlanders were formed by a similar mutilation of the natural scale. By such mutilations, and by various alterations of the notes in tuning the *Vínà,* the number of modes might be augmented indefinitely; and CALLINA'T'HA, admits *ninety* into his system, allowing *six* nymphs, instead of *five,* to each of his musical deities : for *Dí'paca,* which is generally considered as a lost mode (though MIRZA' KHA'N exhibits the notes of it) he substitutes *Panchama;* for *Hindo'la,* he gives us *Vasanta,* or the Spring ; and for *Má'lava, Natanáráyan* or CRISHNA the Dancer; all with scales rather different from those of PA'VAN.

The system of ISWARA which may have had some affinity with the old *Egyptian* musick invented or improved by OSIRIS, nearly resembles that of HANUMAT, but the names and scales are a little varied; in all the systems, the names of the modes are significant, and some of them as fanciful as those of the fairies in the "Midsummer Night's Dream." Forty-eight new modes were added by BHERAT, who *marries* a nymph, thence called *Bháryà*, to each *Putra*, or Son, of a *Rága*, thus admitting, in his musical school, *an hundred and thirty-two manners* of arranging the series of notes.

Had the *Indian* empire continued in full energy for the last two thousand years, religion would, no doubt, have given permanence to systems of musick invented, as the *Hindus* believe, by their Gods, and adapted to mystical poetry : but such have been the revolutions of their government since the time of ALEXANDER, that, although the *Sanscrit* books have preserved the theory of their musical composition, the practice of it seems almost wholly lost (as all the *Pandits* and *Rájas* confess) in *Gaur* and *Magarha*, or the provinces of *Bengal* and *Behar*. When I first read the songs of JAYADE'VA, who has prefixed to each of them the name of the mode in which it was anciently sung, I had hopes of procuring the original musick; but the *Pandits* of the south

referred me to those of the west, and the *Bráhmens* of
the west would have sent me to those of the north;
while they, I mean those of *Népàl* and *Cashmír*,
declared that they had no ancient musick, but im-
agined, that the notes to the *Gítagóvinda* must exist,
if anywhere, in one of the southern provinces, where
the poet was born: from all this I collect that the
art, which flourished in *India* many centuries ago,
has faded for want of due culture, though some
scanty remnants of it may, perhaps, be preserved in
the pastoral roundelays of *Mat'hura* on the loves and
sports of the *Indian* APOLLO.   We must not, therefore, be surprised, if modern performers on the *Vinà*
have little or no *modulation*, or *change of mode*, to
which passionate musick owes nearly all its enchant-
ment; but that the old musicians of *India*, having
fixed on a leading mode to express the *general* character of the song, which they were *translating into
the musical language*, varied that mode, by certain
rules, according to the variation of sentiment or passion in the poetical phrases, and always returned to
it at the close of the air, many reasons induce me to
believe; though I cannot but admit, that their modulation must have been greatly confined by the restriction of certain modes to certain seasons and hours,
unless those restrictions belonged merely to the principal mode.   The scale of the *Vinà*, we find, com-

prized both our *European* modes, and, if some of the notes can be raised a semitone by a stronger pressure on the frets, a delicate and experienced singer might produce the effect of minute enharmonick intervals; the construction of the instrument, therefore, seems to favour my conjecture; and an excellent judge of the subject informs us, that "the open wires are from time to time struck in a manner, that prepares the ear for a change of modulation, to which the uncommonly full and fine tones of those notes greatly contribute"

We may add, that the *Hindu* poets never fail to change the *metre*, which is their *mode*, according to the change of subject or sentiment in the same piece; and I could produce instances of *poetical modulation* (if such a phrase may be used) at least equal to the most affecting modulations of our greatest composers: now the musician must naturally have emulated the poet, as every translator endeavours to resemble his original; and, since each of the *Indian* modes is appropriated to a certain affection of the mind, it is hardly possible, that where the passion is varied, a skilful musician could avoid a variation of the mode. The rules for modulation seem to be contained in the chapters on *mixed modes*, for an intermixture of *Mellár*ì with *To'd*ì and *Saindhav*ì means, I suppose, a transition, however short, from one to another: but the question must remain un-decided, unless we can find in the *Sangitas* a clearer account of modulation, than I am able to produce, or unless we can procure a copy of the *Gîtagôvinda* with the musick, to which it was set, before the time of CALIDAS, in some notation, that may be easily decyphered. It is obvious, that I have not been speaking of a modulation regulated by harmony, with which the *Hindus*, I believe, were unacquainted; though, like the *Greeks*, they distinguish the *con-sonant* and *dissonant* sounds: I mean only such a transition from one series of notes to another, as we see described by the *Greek* musicians, who were ignor-ant of *harmony*, in the modern sense of the word, and perhaps, if they had known it ever so perfectly, would have applied it solely to the support of melody, which alone speaks the language of passion and sentiment.

It would give me pleasure to close this essay with several specimens of old *Indian* airs from the fifth chapter of SO'MA; but I have leisure only to present you with one of them in our own characters accom-panied with the original notes*: I selected the mode of *Vasanta*, because it was adapted by JAYADE'VA himself to the most beautiful of his odes, and be-

---

* It has not been considered necessary to reproduce the Sanskrit notation.—E. R.

cause the number of notes in SO'MA, compared with
that of the syllables in the *Sanscrit* stanza, may lead
us to guess, that the strain itself was applied by the
musician to the very words of the poet.

The words are:

Lelità lavanga latá perisílana cómala malaya samíré,
Madhucara nicara carambita cócila cújita cunja
    cutíré
Víharati heririha sarasa vasanté
Nrītyati yuvati janéna saman sac'hi vitahi janasya
    duranté.

While the soft gale of *Malaya* wafts perfume from
the beautiful clove-plant, and the recess of each
flowery arbour sweetly resounds with the strains of
the *Cócila*, mingled with the murmurs of the honey-
making swarms, HERI dances, O lovely friend, with
a company of damsels in this vernal season; a season
full of delights, but painful to separated lovers.

I have noted SO'MA'S air in the major mode of A,
or *sa*, which, from its gaiety and brilliancy, well ex-
presses the general hilarity of the song; but the sentiment of tender pain, even in a season of delights,
from the remembrance of pleasures no longer attain-
able, would require in our musick a change to the
minor mode; and the air might be disposed in the

form of a rondeau ending with the second line, or even with the third, where the sense is equally full, if it should be thought proper to express by another modulation that *imitative melody*, which the poet has manifestly attempted: the measure is very rapid, and the air should be gay, or even quick, in exact proportion to it.

AN OLD INDIAN AIR.

la li ta la ban ga la ta pe ri si la na co mala am la ya sa

mi re mad huca ra ni ca ra ca ram bi ta co ci la

cu ji ta cun ja cu ti re bi ha ra ti he re ri ha

sa ra sa va san te nrit ya ti yu va ti ja ne na sa man sachi

vi ra hi ja nas ya du ran te

sa ri ga ma pa dha ni sa

The preceding is a strain in the mode of HIN-DO'LA, beginning and ending with the fifth note, *sa*, but wanting *pa*, and *ri*, or the second and sixth: I could easily have found words for it in the *Gita-góvinda*, but the united charms of poetry and musick would lead me too far; and I must now with reluctance bid farewell to a subject, which I despair of having leisure to resume.

BIBLIOGRAPHY.

IX.

Bibliography.

L IST of works in English and French compiled as a guide to students and others interested in Indian music and dance, comprising the names of various works studied by the author, in which reference only is made to the dual arts and matters relating to them.

Tagore (Raja Comm. Sourindro Mohun), "Hindu Music from Various Authors," Calcutta, 1882. The volume is now out of print. Consequently, where possible, details have been given respecting the original publication of the various articles to facilitate reference. The work contains reprints of the following:

"A Treatise on the Music of Hindustan," by Captain N. Augustus Willard Calcutta, 1834.

"Scientific Intelligence," From the "Journal of the Asiatic Society," Volume 25, 1834. A commentary on Willard's treatise.

"On the Musical Modes of the Hindus," by Sir

William Jones. From "Asiatic Researches," Volume 3, 1799. A reprint of the article is contained in the present volume. See page 157, No. VIII of the Appendix.

"Anecdotes of Indian Music," by Sir W. Ouseley. From "Oriental Collections," Volume 1. London, 1797-1800.

"On the Grámas or Musical Scales of the Hindus," by J. D. Paterson. From "Asiatic Researches," Volume 9.

"On the Víná or Indian Lyre," by Francis Fowke. From "Asiatic Researches," Volume 1, 1788.

"Sungeet," by Francis Gladwin. From the "Ain-i-Akbari," Volume 3. Calcutta, 1783.

"The Naqqarahkhána and the Imperial Musicians." Translated from the original Persian by H. Blochmann. From the "Ain-i-Akbari," Volume 1.

"The Music of Hindustan or India," by William C. Stafford.

"Music of the Hindus," by J. Nathan. From "Musurgia Vocalis."

"Catalogue of Indian Musical Instruments," by Col. P. T. French. From the "Proceedings of the Royal Irish Academy," Volume 9, Part 1.

"Music," by Lieut.-Col. James Tod. From the "Annals and Antiquities of Rajast'han," Volume 1. London, 1829.

"Notes on the Musical Instruments of the Nepalese," by A. Campbell. From the "Journal of the Asiatic Society of Bengal," Volume 6, Part 2. Calcutta, 1837.

"Music of Ceylon," by John Davy. From "An Account of the Interior of Ceylon and of its Inhabitants."

"Javanese Music and Dancing," by Crawfurd. From the "History of the Indian Archipelago," Volume 1.

"Musical Instruments," by G. C. M. Birdwood. From "The Industrial Arts of India." Edinburgh, 1880.

"On the Hindu Division of the Octave," by R. H. M. Bosanquet. From the "Proceedings of the Royal Society of London," March to December, 1877.

"Hindu Music," by Sourindro Mohun Tagore. From the "Hindu Patriot," September 7, 1874.

"The Musical Scales of Different Nations," by Carl Engel. From "An Introduction to the Study of National Music." London, 1866.

"The Sáman Chants," by A. C. Burnell. From "The Arsheyabráhmana." Mangalore, 1876.

"The Hindu Theory of Music," by Isaac L. Rice. From "What is Music?"

"The Indian Art of Music," by Sir W. W. Hunter. From "The Imperial Gazetteer of India."

Tagore (Raja Sir Sourindro Mohun), "Universal History of Music." Calcutta, 1896. Now out of print.

———

Day (Captain C. R.), "The Music and Musical Instruments of Southern India and the Deccan." London, Novello, Ewer and Co., and Adam and Charles Black, 1891. Now out of print.

———

Chinnaswami Mudaliyar (A. H.), "Oriental Music in European Notation." Madras, 1893. Now out of print.

———

Fox-Strangways (A. H.), "The Music of Hindostan." Oxford, Clarendon Press, 1914.

———

Clements (E.), "Introduction to the Study of Indian Music." London, Longmans, Green and Co., 1913.

———

Ananda Coomaraswamy, "Indian Music." Reprinted from the "Musical Quarterly," April, 1917, New York.

———

Ananda Coomaraswamy, "The Dance of Siva," Fourteen Indian Essays. New York, 1918.

Krishna Rao (H. P.), "The Psychology of Music." Enlarged edition. Bangalore, 1923.

———

Report of the First All-India Musical Conference held at Baroda in 1916. Baroda, 1917.

Report of the Second All-India Music Conference held at Delhi in 1918. Delhi, 1919.

Report of the Third All-India Music Conference held at Benares in 1919. Benares, 1920.

Report of the Fourth All-India Music Conference held at Lucknow in 1925. Lucknow, 1925.

———

Popley (H. A.), "The Music of India." Calcutta, Association Press, 1921. Heritage of India Series.

———

Nárada, "Sangíta Makaranda." Edited and published in Baroda, 1920.

———

Grosset (J.), "Contribution à l'étude de la musique hindoue." Paris, 1888, Leroux.

———

Atiya Begum Fyzee-Rahamin, "The Music of India." London, Luzac and Co., 1926.

———

Meerwarth (Dr. A. M.), "Guide to the Musical Instruments in the Indian Museum, Calcutta." Government Printing Press, Calcutta, 1917.

Cousins (Mrs. M. E., Mus.B.), "The National Value of Music." An article which appeared in "The Daily Express Annual," 1925.

―――

Thurston (E.), "Ethnographic Notes in Southern India." Madras Government Press, 1906. This work contains many interesting specimens of the verses sung at death ceremonies in Southern India.

―――

Dubois (Abbé J. A.), "Hindu Manners, Customs and Ceremonies," translated from the French by H. K. Beauchamp. Oxford, Clarendon Press, 1897. Contains valuable notes on the temple musicians and dancing girls in India, at the close of the eighteenth century and commencement of the nineteenth century.

―――

Hunter (Sir William Wilson), "The Indian Empire." London, W. H. Allen and Co., 1893. A most useful and comprehensive book of reference, with notes on Indian literature, music, religions, etc.

―――

Da Fonseca (J. N.), "An Historical and Archæological Sketch of the City of Goa." Bombay, 1878. Contains information respecting the musical talent of the Goanese.

Loti (Pierre), " L'Inde (sans les Anglais)." Contains a powerful description of a performance of Indian music at the court of the Maharája of Travancore.

———

Kolatkar, " Dancing in India." An article which appeared in " The Theosophist," April, 1918. Madras.

———

Rothteld (Otto), " Women of India." Bombay, Taraporevala and Sons, 1922. See Chapter VII, " The Dancing Girl."

———

Havelock Ellis, " The Dance of Life." London, Constable and Co., 1923. See Chapter II, " The Art of Dancing."

———

Grellmann (H. M. G.), " Historical Enquiry concerning the Gipsies." Translated into English by Matthew Raper. London, 1787.

———

Hoyland (John), " Historical Survey of the Customs, Habits and Present State of the Gipsies." York, 1816.

———

Mann (Mrs. Maud), " Some Indian Conceptions of Music." Proceedings of the Musical Association, 1911-1912.

Ronaldshay (The Earl of), "Lands of the Thunderbolt." London, Constable and Co., 1923.

Ronaldshay (The Earl of), "India, a Bird's-Eye View." London, Constable and Co., 1924.

Ronaldshay (The Earl of), "The Heart of Aryávarta." London, Constable and Co., 1925.

Tod (Lt.-Col. James), "Annals and Antiquities of Rajast'han." London, 1829. Abridged edition by C. H. Payne, London, 1912.

Havell (E. B.), "Indian Sculpture and Painting." London, John Murray, 1908.

Havell (E. B.), "The Ideals of Indian Art." London, John Murray, 1911

Sambamoorthy (P.), "The Flute." Madras, Indian Music Publishing House, 1927.

N.B.—At the time of going to Press, the Indian Music Publishing House, Madras, announces amongst forthcoming publications a Primer of South Indian Music (in English), a Teacher's Handbook

to the Primer (also in English) and " Musical Types,"
a work dealing with the various types of musical
composition in South Indian music. together with
an account of the leading composers of the various
types of composition (also in English).

INDEX.